TEXAS COWBOYS

D1216854

Outlaw Tom, Riding a Bronk Through the Cactus.
In his youth he learned to "hang and rattle"—anything to keep out of those spines.

(Photograph by Dane Coolidge)

DANE COOLIDGE

TEXAS COWBOYS

Foreword by Owen Ulph

With Photographs by the Author

The University of Arizona Press
Tucson, Arizona

About the Author

DANE COOLIDGE (1873 – 1940) was an itinerant photographer and writer who traveled throughout the American West, recording native wildlife and the developing frontier. He was the author of numerous magazine pieces and books, perhaps the best known of which are *Arizona Cowboys*, *California Cowboys*, and *Texas Cowboys*, all available from the University of Arizona Press.

THE UNIVERSITY OF ARIZONA PRESS
First Printing 1985

"Dane Coolidge: An Appreciation," by Owen Ulph, originally appeared as "A Dedication to Dane Coolidge, 1873–1940" in the Spring 1981 issue of *Arizona and the West*, and is reprinted by permission.

Library of Congress Cataloging-in-Publication Data

Coolidge, Dane, 1873–1940.
Texas cowboys.

Reprint. Originally published: New York: Dutton, 1937.
1. Cowboys—West (U.S.)—History—20th century.
2. Ranch life—West (U.S.)—History—20th century.
3. Ranch life—Southwest, New—History—20th century.
I. Title.
F596.C76   1985   978'.03   85-16333

ISBN 0-8165-0947-6 (pbk).

CONTENTS

ILLUSTRATIONS

ILLUSTRATIONS

DANE COOLIDGE:
AN APPRECIATION

"To the young man seeking adventure I could give no better advice than to get a moderate sized hat, a pair of overalls and a horse and strike out into the cow country. If he has the nerve with which I have endowed Bat Wing Bowles he will win out, if he hasn't he will get the adventures anyway." When Dane Coolidge promulgated this romantic advice during a newpaper interview in the spring of 1914 it was reasonably sound. Coolidge had turned forty and had achieved success as a scholar and novelist by following that same course of action, but not at anyone's suggestion. Supplementing a gambler's audacity with logic and respect for experience, Coolidge made his own decisions. Like the protagonist of his novel, *Bat Wing Bowles*, he was an easterner who came west adequately supplied with "nerve" to a degree that prompted range-bred acquaintances to describe him later as "a feller with a speck of heck in his neck."

1

Certainly the West never exposed Coolidge to culture shock. He was only four years old when he migrated. His father, a New England farmer of salty independence, moved the family to Riverside, California, from Natick, Massachusetts, where Dane, his second son, had been born on March 24, 1873. When Dane returned to Massachusetts twenty years later to do graduate work in biology, he was an "outlander" himself who found the atmosphere of Harvard stultifying and the *milieu* he was obliged to share with relatives who had remained rooted with the ivy scarcely less so. That one of those relatives—a cousin a year older than he—eventually became the thirtieth president of the United States, was a fact to which Dane apparently remained indifferent.

The Coolidge family did not wallow in green and gold velvet. A citrus ranch provided acceptable status, but not wealth, at a time when agriculture, despite its place in the sun, occupied a shadowy corner of the economy. When Dane's mother died before he finished high school, he became the family chamberlain and took over the exchequer, leaving ranch duties mostly to his father and elder brother. The experience impressed him with the fluidity and inflammability of money. Thereafter he was always shrewdly alert to secure the mercurial tender against the

2

merciless laws of gravitation and combustion. Herein lies a clue to his eventual preference for potentially lucrative fiction over less marketable scholarship.

After graduating from Riverside High School in 1894, Dane enrolled at Stanford, a neophyte educational institution established, according to legend, to provide opportunites for higher learning for young persons long on character and intelligence, but short on pecuniary resources. Dane worked as a hasher "serving 20 women, 3 times a day for $7.50 per month and leftovers." During the summers he supplemented this scant income by traveling over southern and Baja California, Nevada, Arizona, and northern Mexico, collecting specimens for the university's natural history collection, the British Museum, the National Zoological Park, and other wildlife mausoleums. As a boy, Dane had thoroughly explored Riverside County's extensive wastelands before they were buried beneath acres of macadam and concrete, and in the process he had become a skilled hunter, trapper, amateur taxidermist, and self-trained naturalist. In the summer of 1896 he collected a thousand bird's eggs which he sold to museums for 2½¢ each. As a "Cherry Cow" puncher once remarked, "That's a helluva lot of eggs to suck for twenty-five bucks!"

3

Although Dane's correspondence indicates what might be considered an obsessive concern for money, he was in reality only an incorrigible accountant. He never complained or despaired. Instead, his financial philosophy was pre-welfare, exuberant, Darwinian, speculative, and typically Western—as expressed in the enviable assurance of the late Mike Todd, "I've often been broke, but I've never been poor."

In high school and college Dane was devoted to literature and during his senior year at Stanford, he became editor of the student publication, *The Sequoia*, succeeding his mentor, Edward Maslin Hulme, subsequently appointed to the chair in Medieval and Renaissance History at the university. Hulme was a romantic scholar and Coolidge a scholarly romantic. Together these mavericks crusaded unsuccessfully against fraternities and other vestiges of tribalism in an era extolling rugged individualism.

After graduating from Stanford in 1898, Coolidge resumed his impromptu profession as a "field collector," obtaining a contract to stalk the European hinterlands for imprudent fauna. While in London, he observed that Old World wildlife specimens were not alone in manifesting odd characteristics. "Some of the people here speak the same language with us," he wrote, "but

4

I cannot understand the boys in the street or half the market people." The estranged exile re-crossed the Atlantic, sampled Harvard and found it worse than London. There remained only one salvation for a sane man. Dane abandoned Harvard with a bouquet of B's after one year and came home—not simply to the geographical west, but to the *real* West—Arizona at the close of the century.

The native's return was not made entirely without concessions to social orthodoxy. According to the commencement program of Riverside High School, Dane had delivered a minor elocutionary masterpiece of self-fantasy entitled "The Professional Bachellor." Twelve years of intellectual and equestrian vagabonding terminated in 1906, when he married Mary Elizabeth Burroughs Roberts. The two had met during Dane's student years at Stanford, where Mary had been an associate professor of sociology. Later, as Mrs. Coolidge, she would head the sociology department at Mills College. Although Dane accepted the "double harness," urban domesticity and a permanent domicile, neither he nor his adventuresome wife abandoned the active life of field research. Together they collaborated on *The Navajo Indians* and *The Last of the Seris*, based on studies conducted jointly while living among the respective tribes in Arizona and Baja California. "It seems to me that one can do more brilliant work in the highly stimulating climate of Arizona and I go there for material," Coolidge explained, "but when I want a quiet place to work I go back to the fog belt in Berkeley." Coolidge spent over thirty intermittent years in the Southwest and two in Wyoming reviewing the case of Tom Horn, executed in 1903 for the alleged murder of the fourteen-year-old son of a sodbuster who had perversely imported sheep into cow country.

Clear perspective on Coolidge's character and personality is possible only through an account of the conflicts he experienced as an author of popular fiction. He was, after all, a writer of "horse opera." In 1910 Coolidge published his first novel, *Hidden Water*, set in the Four Peaks area of the Salt River country. His career as a writer of westerns thus began less than decade following publication of Owen Wister's *The Virginian* and Andy Adams's *Log of a Cowboy*, two novels which established the eviternal schism in the tradition of the cowboy story. While grudgingly conceding Wister's literary merits, Coolidge reserved his unqualified admiration for Adams. Dane had spent much of that decade among cowboys on the "Cherry Cow" spread in Arizona, and

6

the association enhanced his regard for authenticity. Most of his competitors, hawkers of what W. H. Hutchinson has dubbed "the commercial western, the oater in all its mutant forms," aroused Coolidge's scorn. He could not accept publishers' dogmas about "market demand" and consumer taste. He recognized the value of an intriguing plot, action, suspense, and sudden shifts in fortune, but he was convinced that these ingredients of a good yarn could be retained without sacrificing plausibility of situation and fidelity of characterization.

Dane was a realistic as well as a scholarly romantic. He was dedicated to ascertainable facts and maintained his own clipping bureau and "data bank" to supply him with accurate materials for his books. He was also an excellent cowboy photographer, who claimed that he "only used the camera as a disguise for gathering material for writing." He eventually contracted with *Western Horseman* to exchange his photographs for advertising space for his novels.

As a humanist, Coolidge was sensitive to the aesthetic and dramatic dimensions of life and cognizant of the importance of initiative and imagination to creativity. His writing, filled with incongruities, reflects his aspiration to synchronize these ostensibly incompatible goals. To a great

7

extent his double vision explains why the forty-five books he published between 1910 and 1940 have remained out of print and why their author is virtually unknown today. Coolidge's insistence upon authenticity and his uncompromising disregard for conventionality undermined the marketability of his "westerns," while his inventive disposition rendered his works of nonfiction academically suspect.

The apprehension that Coolidge wasted a fine talent is haunting. Certainly he possessed capabilities that surpassed his performance. Evidence of this surfaces even in his most trivial work. He could not suppress his irreverent wit or his superiority of mind—qualities that make reading his formula-racked extravaganzas still rewarding, although not to gunsmoke addicts.

Coolidge, however, did not entirely reject his birthright. In addition to the studies in social anthropology which he produced in collaboration with his wife, he wrote three deceptively simple, but truly acute works of nonfiction: *Texas Cowboys*, *Arizona Cowboys*, and *California Cowboys*, all now available in paperback from the University of Arizona Press. At the end of his life he was preparing a disquisition on the Mexican *vaquero*, the outline for which demonstrates the exacting, precise, and inclusive nature of his method of inquiry. Whenever he took liberties with the code of the scholar, he did so deliberately—and for a purpose. He never spun his biases, as many academics are wont to do, on a bogus scientific loom. Dane Coolidge *understood* the West. By the time of his death on August 8, 1940, that West had few survivors.

Readers continue to prefer "The West that Wasn't" to the West that was. Coolidge attempted to reverse the order of preference. With all his stratagems and his partiality for fast-action fiction over academic treatises, he never ceased to be a thoughtful, erudite, civilized gentleman whose insights into the nomadic components of frontier culture merit greater recognition than they have been accorded.

OWEN ULPH

TEXAS COWBOYS

SNARING SHADOWS

WITH far more justification than Charley Russell, the Western artist, I can say I am not a cowboy. I never even pretended to be one, or I wouldn't have got the pictures I did. Being a cowboy calls for a lifetime of training—and something is likely to happen to you if you admit you know how to ride. So I always wore a small-sized hat and told them I was just a photographer, and unless they gave me a gentle horse I was liable to fall off and break my camera.

A cowboy likes nothing better than to have his picture taken, mounted on his top horse; so they always gave me a good one, and I took most of my photographs from the saddle. Either that or down on one knee in the corral—and I was safer on the horse. Because when a bronk is pitching he will run over anything; and I often had to rise up and fly, just when the picture was getting right. But I stayed with it long enough to get a few good ones—the rest I took from the fence.

Even at that I was not a regular photographer. I seldom sold any pictures and just took my camera along as a bluff, so they would let me follow the round-up. I was really scouting around for story material, although I never talked about that. I announced that I was a photographer and a good one; and if I promised a man a picture, he got it. Some thought I was a traveling picture-man, selling them three for a dime, and treated me despitefully; but, when they found I wouldn't sell to people I didn't like, they were sorry—or that's what I hope.

My first work was in Arizona, with Mexican outfits or Americans working California style, and I still remember how we stared when the first Texas cowboy struck town. He had dropped off a cattle-train and wore his pants inside his boots, which had long straps hanging down on both sides so he could pull them on in a hurry.

12

His hat was bigger than ours and he wore huge clanky spurs, such as the *conquistadores* brought over from Spain, along with the horses and cows.

The cattle business all goes back to Spain—it is only a question of how far. There is a California style of working cattle and a Texas style, the California style dating first. California, Arizona, New Mexico, and most of the country west of the Rockies still cling to the old Spanish ways; but the Texans, having a brushy country, worked out a way of their own. First of all they developed the heavy wing shaps, made from bull hide to stand off the prickly pears and thorny catclaws and mesquite. Then they learned to separate their reins, so they would not get hung up by the bridle; and, probably for the same reason, they gave up the cumbersome Spanish bits and adopted something plain.

The double-cinch, so characteristic of Texas, was probably the product of brush-riding—and they had some bad cattle to deal with. The Texas longhorns were a breed by themselves and when a man chased one out of the "pears"

13

and tied to him he wanted that saddle to *hold.*
Otherwise he would land in such a mess of
thorns and stickers that it would take him two
days to pick them out. So in their youth they
learned to "hang and rattle," grabbing any-
where with their spurs when they had to and
choking the horn—anything to keep out of
those spines.

As a class they are better riders than the California style cowboys but not so good at roping.
Most Texans use a thirty-five-foot maguey or
sea-grass rope, tied to the horn; while the Californians swing a rawhide *reata,* perhaps sixty
feet long and take their turns around the horn.
The Texans whirl a small loop, on account of
the brush; but when they tie to a critter they
stay with him "till hell's no more." They have
to, or lose their saddles and maybe get "drug"
through the cactus. So they need all the help
they can get—a double-cinch to hold on the saddle, split reins that won't catch in the trees, and
heavy shaps to stand off the thorns.

Most people think of Texas as a land of
boundless plains—and so it is, in the north; but

the western part, I know, is rough and spotted with cactus, and the southern ranges run to cactus-pears and mesquite. There are wide plains between the thickets; but the Texans are brush cowboys, as shown by their rigging, which they keep wherever they go. Eastern Texas, according to the punchers, is given over to cotton and corn; and their favorite term of reproach is to call a man a cotton-picker. It expresses their scorn for agriculture in general, and "row-crops" in particular.

Yet the cotton-picking farmers have taken their country; and, since about 1900, the cowboys have been moving west. Then, about 1910, the big cattlemen were routed out and came west to look for new range. Having sold out their holdings in the Panhandle and Central Texas they had money in both hands; and they took over New Mexico like a foreign invasion, shipping out the native stock and bringing in Texas cattle.

Southeast Arizona was next, and they shipped through to Imperial Valley and over the Line into Mexico. Montana and Wyoming had long been their stamping-ground, but they took it all over again; until now every cow-puncher you see is a Texan, except a few old-timers who are left. But while they got most of the northern range, when they moved further west they ran into the cowman's Nemesis—sheep.

There has been many a bloody battle fought for possession of the western range, and the sheep have always won. They reproduce twice as fast as cattle, mature four times as quick, and the wool-clip alone pays the expense of taking care of them. Legally the sheepmen have equal rights in feeding off the Government domain; and, if they can't get those rights peacefully, they know how to get them the other way.

The cattlemen were fighting a losing battle when, about 1916, Nature took a hand in the game. There was a drouth, and more drouths; and, after twenty more-or-less-dry years, the range cattle business was done for. Millions of cows are still left, but they are all under fence and the day of the cowboy is past. The best of them are contest-riders and ropers, or working on some dude-ranch, but the bold riders from

Texas who used to rule the Western plains have disappeared like the Indians.

After snaring their shadows for thirty-five years, I am bringing out these few pictures to show what a cowboy used to look like.

CHAPTER I

THE CHERRYCOW OUTFIT

THEY are a breed by themselves, these Texans,
and still in the cattle business—where there are
any cattle left. But twenty-eight years ago I saw
as fine a bunch of them as ever worked a range—
the Cherrycow outfit on the San Carlos Indian
Reservation in Arizona. Every man a straight
Texan, with split reins and double-cinch; and
they called the afternoon "this evening."

It was open range, probably the last in the
United States, with all sheepmen and nesters
barred. There were no fences, no roads, no
wagon-tracks even, and it took me five days from
the time I left San Carlos till I caught up with
the cowboys. They were on their way back,
crossing five hundred head of cattle at Black
River—and the cook had quit six weeks before.

Their food had consisted of bread, beef, and coffee, with the beef and bread either burned or raw; and when they saw me they gave a cheer. I had come in with the new cook.

Sam had been out eight days, and lost all the time. He had trailed them from the Gila to where they had crossed Black River on a raft—and left it on the other side. Then he had come back to the horse-camp on Blue River and together we had proceeded to Black River Ferry—with Uncle Hal, the horse-camp man, for guide. After a four-bit meal at the ferryman's cabin we were lying in the shade watching them sweat when one of the cowboys spied us.

"Hey, Dad!" he shouted to the wagon-boss, who was having a hard time with his cattle, "there's your new cook over there, laying under a tree! Sam, you lazy haound, come over hyer and cook us some supper!"

"You go to hell, you so-and-so," retorted Sam. "Cook your own supper!" And, strange as it may seem, they did.

Their makeshift cook for the past six weeks had been a cowboy calling himself Cherrycow

Charley. He had quit three times and the boss had raised his pay until he was getting sixty dollars a month, cooking worse and worse all the time so someone would kick on the grub. Then, of course, the kicker would have to cook; but the cowboys were all wise. They kept their mouths shut until Sam appeared, and Charley's last meal was terrible. We crossed over on the ferry that evening and Sam ate with the rest; but the next morning, when he took hold, the beef was tender, the biscuits light, the coffee strong, and Sam and I were made much of.

At the ferryman's cabin I had met Henry S. Boice, the new owner, who had just bought out J. V. Vickers, and he had told me to go ahead and get my pictures; but it was coming in with Sam that made me welcome. After a three-days rain and a month on the northern range the cowboys were a hard-looking lot, with their ragged overalls and jumpers and a shaggy growth of beard. They were dog-tired too, and ready to strike; and old Dad Hardiman, the wagon-boss, was in bad with them.

Contrary to their judgment he had decided

to cross the herd when they first hit the river, hoping that the thirsty ones behind would shove the leaders in and make them swim across. It was noon and his hands were hot and dusty and starving for something to eat; but, after holding up the herd to think it over, Dad finally rose in his stirrups and shouted:

"Let 'em go!"

The men in front gave way and the leaders trotted down with their tongues out; but, though the cowboys in the rear whooped and swung their ropes, the great mass of tired animals, instead of rushing forward, barely got off a walk. Then it was that Dad, who was in a high state of nerves, began to shout contradictory orders.

"Turn 'em back!" he yelled, riding down to the point. "No, let 'em go!" he hollered, waving his hat to the dragmen; and, while he raged up and down, the disgruntled cowboys pushed the cattle steadily forward and shoved them into the river. At the shore the leaders lowered their heads to drink, others crowded in and horned them on. They edged out further and further,

22

still drinking, until suddenly they slumped off into deep water and began to swim. But, seeing no place to land on the other side, the leaders drifted down with the current and came ashore where they had started from.

After a futile effort to drive them in again, the boss finally gave orders to let the cattle drink and called on Cherrycow Charley for dinner. There was a short wait while the cowboys filled up with beef and bread and then, after changing mounts, they went at it by day's works. Cutting out about fifty head at a time they jumped them over a low bank into the river and finally steered them across. It was sundown by the time the last animal was over and, wet and bedraggled, the cowboys rode back to where Charley had done his worst.

But as the first cup of coffee took the edge off their grouch, their unrestrained Texas humor burst forth. Old Dad had worked harder than any of them but his plans had gone wrong, and the memory of his contradictory orders still irked them.

"Let 'em go!" observed an iron-faced puncher,

solemnly spearing a hunk of beef from the oven.

"Turn 'em back!" shrilled another, coming in on the play; and a rumble of sardonic laughter passed around the circle of cowboys, sitting cross-legged in the outer darkness. Dad sat by the fire, supping his coffee and peering out from under his hat, but no one was worrying about him. They were short-handed already and fifty miles from town, and they knew they would not get fired.

"Sho, sho, boys," pleaded another voice, boldly mimicking the boss, "don't yell so loud— it only skeers 'em! Oh Lawzy, Lawzy, I'm so wor'ied!" And then the whole bunch laughed until you could hear them a mile.

They are a hard outfit to handle, these Texas cowboys, and when there is heavy work afoot the boss expects to take a lot. There is none of your English deference in a cow-camp, and none of your Eastern "Yes, sirs," either. "Allright" or "Uh-huh" was the best Dad ever got when he gave an order; and if they were compelled to refer to him as the boss they were careful to say "the straw-boss", although Hardi-

24

man had been in command for nine years and could fire any one of them.

It is part of the wild and boisterous independence of the West, this studied disregard for authority; and, while a cowboy will do a tremendous amount of work in the line of duty, his untamed spirit will not permit him to "supe" for anybody. The only Mister in the Cherrycow outfit was an old, white-haired man, a little broken by the month of hard riding but silent and uncomplaining. No matter what the occasion, there was never a cowboy too busy to put the handle on Mr. King's name; and when he had anything to say they shut up and let him say it. But the rest of the time there was a rapid-fire of frontier witticisms that was calculated to get under the thickest hide and leave drummers' tales badly faded.

Unrestrained of speech they were, like the Greek heroes of Homer; and, until the last cow is corralled, the hard-riding cowboy is going to be unrestrained. For cow-punching is not a job to bring out the minor Christian virtues. It calls for those Spartan qualities which, though they

25

rise from man's baser nature, make a steer throw a crook into his tail and fly.

But, though they made bold to josh the boss and on all occasions to "run off at the head," there was one man, newly come into camp, whom the punchers left strictly alone. That was the cook. It had taken the Range Boss six weeks to round up Mr. Elkins and get him to take the job and, except for a fight he got into, he would not have come at all. Some drunken brute at Globe had chased him around the wagon with a butcher-knife until he got tired of it, grabbed up the double-tree and laid him out with one blow. The judge had given Sam two weeks in jail, but his opponent drew a month; and it was to avoid killing him when he got out that Sam had taken to the range.

He was one of the best round-up cooks in the West, having worked at it off and on for twenty years; but, after routing them out at four in the morning and listening to them talk, he had lost all respect for cowboys. Since he drew twice their pay and did twice their work he had some excuse for his pride, and good round-up cooks

CROSSING BLACK RIVER.

The leaders, though crowded into the water by the thirsty animals behind, are turning back.

(Photograph by Dane Coolidge)

SAM, THE COOK, WITH HIS PACK-OUTFIT AND DUTCH OVENS.
The first so-and-so that kicks on the grub will be told where to go.

(Photograph by Dane Coolidge)

were scarce. Sam would wake up at three A.M., look at the stars, and scratch a match to see if his watch was keeping time. Then he would get out his sour-dough "kag" and mix up a breadpan full of dough; after which he would slice off steaks, set his ovens over the coals, and heave more wood on the fire.

At four o'clock he would let out a long yell: *"Eeeee-yow!"*—all that was left after many years of service of "Git up!"—and fly at the job of serving a hot breakfast for twenty. Then he would wash up the dishes, generally with the aid of a flunky, and, with all kinds of help from the cowboys, pack the grub and his whole cooking outfit on the mules. They would see him off before starting on the circle; and at ten or eleven o'clock, when they brought in the cattle, he would be camped up ahead somewhere, all ready with another meal.

The biscuits were always light, the beef cooked just right; and, the morning after Charley quit the job, the Cherrycow outfit was happy. They had been on short rations for a month, and Dad Hardiman earned a cheer when he told Mr. Elkins he could order all the grub he wanted. Just write it down on a piece of paper and he would send a man in for it. Old Juan, the Mexican packer, had twenty burros in his train and, by the time we got to the horse-camp on Blue River, he would have the order *there*.

Immediately the boys' imaginations ran riot and for the next three days they could talk of nothing but stewed fruit, puddings, mush, and milk from the little tin cow. But at some previous time in Sam's career some miscreant had evidently spoken disparagingly of his cooking and he did not warm to their praise. From long catering to the fickle appetite his face had become set in cynical lines, and when any man spoke well of the food he looked up with an embittered smile. He never said much, and the few stories he did tell were obviously intended to point a moral. They were all about men who had kicked on his grub, and invariably ended as follows:

"And I said to the blankety-blank: 'Well, if you don't like it you know what you can do, don't you?' And that shut him up, damned quick."

It was a happy day indeed for the careworn punchers when, five days later, in the midst of a general horse-shoeing and uncocking of bronks, the long pack-train came stringing in from San Carlos, loaded down with supplies for the cook. There were new ovens and a proper pot-hook, made by the San Carlos blacksmith, a little keg for sour dough; and then, oh joy, two cases of condensed milk and a mule-load of Cream of Wheat.

To make the gala day complete the boys killed a fat young beef, and with the suet Sam made a great "pud" in his new sixteen-inch oven. It was a wonderful pudding, full of raisins, richly flavored with vinegar and spices. Everybody came back twice for more; and, as the last man leaned back and sighed, the embittered look left Sam's face. There was good eating after that, and the first man that kicked on his grub would have got run out of camp.

CHAPTER II

A FINE LARGE COUNTRY

THEY had a large range to ride over, these cowboys from Texas, about the biggest in the West. The White Mountain or San Carlos Reserve is approximately eighty miles square, giving it an area of over six thousand square miles, besides several hundred more of straight up and straight down. The first cattle were brought in to feed the soldiers and their unfriendly wards, the Apaches; and the Chiricahua Cattle Company soon began to run its herds along the Gila—its name being shortened to Cherrycow.

It is a fine, large country for three thousand Indians to run over, but on account of their unfortunate dispositions the Apaches had never been allowed to run very far. And, since it was necessary to keep the cattle near at hand, the

31

Government soon began to hire out the range to beef contractors. The soldiers were gone from San Carlos now and some of the Indians had cattle of their own; but the custom established twenty-five years before, when Vickers brought up the first CCC cattle from his ranch in the Chiricahua Mountains, still prevailed.

For every cow-brute over a year old that was taken in the spring round-up, the Company paid the United States one dollar; and this yearly toll, together with the money paid by the Double Circles, the Wine Glass and the Hat outfits, was supposed to be turned over to the Indians. But for some reason or other it never got back to them and the Apaches, who know nothing of departmental red tape, decided it was better to kill a fat two-year-old whenever they got meat-hungry.

This form of direct tax, which was frowned upon by the authorities, made a slight difference in the size of the Three C beef shipments. But every range has its drawbacks and, to balance the losses from Indians and loafer wolves, there was the greater compensation that all sheepmen and nesters were barred. The government would not accept bids to graze sheep on what was already a cattle range, and no white men other than cowboys were allowed to live on the Reservation. The result was a land covered with cattle as far as the eye could see; and only the big round-up outfits, with their pack-trains and trailing bands of horses, broke the solitude of the wilderness.

What Texas had been forty years before, San Carlos was in 1909. The Cherrycow outfit even went them one better for, on account of the many miles of malpai lava, they had given up the use of a chuck-wagon. The men that rode for the Company had to lash their beds on broken-down cow ponies every time they broke camp, and the wagon-boss, despite his title, had to do without a wagon.

It was a real old Texas outfit, one of the last in the United States, and from the Range Boss in San Carlos down to the cook's flunky dragging up wood, they all spoke the soft dialect of Texas, dropped most of their r's and called the afternoon this evening.

Henry S. Boice, the new owner, had for many years been General Manager of the XIT Cattle Company in Texas, until the wire-trust and the nesters got in their deadly work and fenced the whole Panhandle off. At the present time, so the Cherrycow boys informed me, it presented a peaceful, pastoral scene with haystacks, clotheslines and all that. There were no Texans left in Texas—all were out West, punching cows.

There were twenty men in the round-up outfit, and they worked the cattle the year around. The year before, while making their reservation count, they had gathered four thousand head in one morning; and for an ordinary branding they would throw two thousand head onto the cutting grounds, change horses and cut out the cows and calves before noon. In the dead of winter, when the upper range was covered with snow and the lower ground would bog a saddle-blanket, there came a lull in the work. The best men went on station, to keep the Indians from stealing beef, or broke horses on the lower Gila; while the poorest rode the chuckline, traveling from ranch to ranch, living on

34

A FINE, LARGE COUNTRY.
The Cherrycow range was one vast rock-patch, but it produced thousands of cattle.
(Photograph by Dane Coolidge)

RUSTY BILL, THE BRONK-TWISTER.
He hasn't been on a gentle horse in two years.
(Photograph by Dane Coolidge)

cigarettes and Western hospitality until the round-ups began in the spring.

When I set out from San Carlos in search of the elusive Cherrycow outfit the poppies and Indian paint-brushes were flowering along the Gila; but before I caught up with them I was in the shadow of giant cedars and a big movement of cattle was on. The Vickers Company had been suffering heavy losses around Fort Apache and on the north side of Black River, and the first thing Henry Boice did was to order the cattle shifted around.

"If I've got to keep those Indians in beef," he said, "I'm not going to feed them my Herefords."

So he gathered all the rough, longhorned steers below the line and shoved them across the river; after which he rounded up the best of his northern cows and moved them down to his lower range. It was the tail end of this drive which we had witnessed at Black River, a wide and turbulent stream; after which we drifted south in the direction of the horse-camp, to get a change of mounts.

35

The Three C outfit kept about five hundred head of wire-grass horses in its "pasture," on the lava-covered mesa above Blue River—a high, level plain, cut off on three sides by abysmal canyons and only fenced at the upper end. That fence was set on top of the ground, the posts held up by piles of rocks and boulders, and if a band of horses had ever run into it they would have knocked it flat for a mile. But a range horse is deathly afraid of barbed-wire and, no matter how bronco they were, they always turned in time. There was everything in this pasture from a broken-down pack animal to a man-eating outlaw, but most of the horses were young and sound—only a little wild. They had been raised in the Sulphur Spring Valley, on the Company's lower range, and the cowboys surely needed a change.

"Yes, sir," said Uncle Hal Young, the horse-camp man, "those boys are *afoot.* They've only got three horses apiece."

The pack animals laid down grunting before their loads could be cast loose; and the declining sun cast shadows between the ribs of every horse in the remuda. And the saddle-horses, though they scampered like cats over the overlasting malpai rocks, held their heads to one side as they ran to watch for the slash of the quirt. It was time the horse-changing began.

The horse-camp and corrals were beneath the bluffs of Blue River Canyon, among the wild walnuts and sycamores, and early the next morning twenty men rode up the trail and rimmed out on the pasture side. As they passed through the gate, which had been set deep with crowbars, a few horsemen galloped off along the edges of the precipice which served the purpose of a fence, and soon a long line of horses appeared, spread out from brink to brink. But, before they struck the fence, waiting cowboys popped up unexpectedly and with a thunderous rumble of hoofs the immense troop swept back across the cutting grounds, their manes shaken to the wind and their tails held up like banners.

Not a horse there but knew the purport of this raid and, at the first attempt to hold them up, there was a resistless dash for freedom. The leader of them all was a high-headed black and as he went through the line like a war-horse the cowboys cursed him by name. It was old Dan Patch, once the top horse of the outfit until a fool horse-breaker got hold of him and rode him with whip and spur. He had come in, raked and bleeding, after piling his rider in the rocks; but since that time, for nearly two years, he had remained unridden and untamed. But as he led the herd away a single horseman, riding with quirt and spurs, outran the best of them and turned the stampede back.

Once more the band of outlaws charged down on the fence as if they would lay it flat, then circled past the herd of gentle horses which had been held up on the cutting grounds; but their untamed spirits scorned the thought of servitude and once more they rushed the line. A dozen times they broke through and ran on, but each time a man spurred after them and brought them back to the gate. Then, as the constant racing back and forth wore the weaker animals down, they came to a reluctant halt and stood gazing over each other's backs at the cowboys they knew all too well.

38

There was no hardier outfit of punchers in the United States than the men who were gathered there that day. Every man a Tehanno born—and he was supposed to be an A1 rider or he would never have taken the job. But when it came horse-changing time there were only three cowboys who acknowledged that they could ride—Rusty Bill and Jess Fears, the hired bronco-twisters, and Bishop Greenhouse who was redheaded and foolish.

The rest, while admitting a certain proficiency in the past, claimed to be all shot to pieces inside; and observed furthermore that the Cherry horses were the snakiest bunch of man-killers in Arizona, to a blank-blanked certainty. When you go to a Wild West Show the man in the polka-dot shirt and woolly shaps only laughs when his horse throws a buck-jump and comes down stiff-legged. But he is paid to laugh —remember that. Out on the range a cowboy generally figures that he earns his forty dollars a month without doing any rough-riding, and he strikes for a gentle mount.

But the Cherrycow horses were known to be

wild ones, bred in the open and broke in a week, and in order to get men to ride them the management paid its top hands forty-five. Even then there was no great jam of rough-riders, and most of the heavy work was done by the professional horse-breakers, who drew down fifty dollars a month. So, when it came to the horse-cut and Uncle Hal rode out with his little book, the Three C men didn't really expect much. All they asked was a good night-horse, another one halfway gentle—and of course, three bronks. Every man got three bronks, some of them got four; and Rusty Bill, the twister, said he hadn't been on a gentle horse for more than two years.

They were beautiful creatures, those wild half-mustang cow horses, full of an agile grace and swiftness, but bronco to the tips of their ears. If they could have been caught up and gentled many of them would have made pets, but on the range there was nothing for it but the rope and spur and quirt. As they wove about under the dust-cloud—bays and roans, sorrels and blacks, pintos, palominos and grullas—even the cowboys got them confused and asked the twisters which was which. But there was one man, sitting quietly on his fleabitten gray, who knew them as a mother knows her children.

CHAPTER III

THE HORSE-CHANGING

UNCLE Hal Young was too tender-hearted to be a cowboy—he believed in a hereafter for any man who abused a horse—and, while it was his business to give out the mounts, he did the best he could for them. The only man who had a stand-in with Uncle Hal was the one who was good to his horses, and cruel riders found themselves outfitted with a string of snakes that would scare a Rodeo hand, and all their protests disregarded.

Riding along the edge of the herd with the wagon-boss, who was worried because he couldn't give every man in the outfit the five best horses, Uncle Hal listened to him with an indulgent smile, meanwhile scanning the sea of heads and backs for the particular mounts he

43

wanted. Then he drew out his notebook, the alternate pages of which contained testimonials from grateful patent-medicine dopes, and called up the number one cowboy.

"Well, Bill," he said, "I've got you down for Three Spots, Peanuts, Aleman, Cream of Wheat, and Scrapper—is that all right?"

"Sure," responded Bill. "But say, I noticed old Scrapper is a little lame yet in that off shoulder. He fell with me last time, you know."

"Well, you take Black River then, and we'll let him run," said Hal with a kindly smile; but when, later on, Mr. Rough-rider showed up for a mount, he drew old Scrapper for a certainty. It was an anxious time for old Dad, the wagon-boss, and already he could see himself short-handed; but Uncle Hal had a long memory for spur-marks and bruised heads and if anybody got mad and quit he wanted it to be a rough hand.

As soon as he had assigned the first string of horses, two pairs of cowboys were sent into the herd to cut them out. To stop their mad flight, the tired-out remuda and the steady-going old

Uncle Hal, the Horse-Camp Man, has it out with the Wagon-Boss, who is worried because he can't give every man in the outfit the five best horses.

(Photograph by Dane Coolidge)

CATCHING OUT A NEW MOUNT.

(Photograph by Dane Coolidge)

pack-animals were driven out to serve as a hold-up, and when Three Spots and Peanuts were edged out of the herd they were stampeded across the open and into the smaller bunch.

Often some quiet horse would recognize a friend in the hold-up herd and trot over to join him, but most of them had to be cut out by hard riding and profanity; and as outlaw after outlaw improved the opportunity to make a last break for freedom, the turmoil grew into a riot. But a cowboy's life is a hectic proposition at best, and to the men of the Cherrycow the hard riding was only a part of the day's work. By noon, through some miracle, the horse-cut was complete; and as the main herd scampered away across the pasture the cut was driven down the steep trail and thrown into the round corral at the bottom of the canyon.

The Blue River corral was large and strong, built of peeled poles, with cedar posts at the gate; and, while the boys were eating dinner across the creek, the two hundred horses ran round and round in it as if they were stamping

45

out grain for an Old Mexico *ranchero*. When the hands came back to begin their shoeing, the trees were already powdered with fine dust and the corral was completely hidden.

The first man that entered the pen held his rope low, but there was something ominous about his pose and all gave way before him. As he marked down his horse and sidled towards him the great treadmill was set in motion again, the animals on the sides running behind him as he advanced until, when he reached the center, he was surrounded by a great circle of horses, thundering round with the resistless power of an avalanche. Every animal in the band was haunted by a nervous apprehension of that sudden, snake-like cast, but the horse that felt the eye of his master upon him went wild with terror. Fighting his way through the press he jammed himself in behind his mates, while the old plugs and pack animals, knowing they were not wanted, plodded cheerfully along on the inside.

At last, flipping the rope along the ground in front of him, the cowboy twitched it back and

46

made his throw. The loop settled over a horse's head—some horse's—and the next moment was jerked out of his hands. Then the treadmill turned into a wild stampede and, as the pace quickened into a gallop, shoots of dirt belched out through the holes in the fence and the cowboy was swallowed up in dust. He may have been a good cowhand, but in this case his judgment was bad; and, after a futile attempt to pick up his rope, he passed up the job and motioned to the bronco-twisters.

Tall, lithe and quick-eyed, they had sat on the fence with the rest, whooping and laughing; but now they wiped the smile off their faces and dropped down into the corral. For five dollars extra a month they had agreed to handle every bad horse and uncock every bronk—provided, always, that they were asked—but their reward was more in the grim sense of mastery than in the money paid. They were the top cowhands, and every man who called on them for help paid tribute to their prowess.

Trailing their ropes behind them they advanced from two sides upon the horse who was

47

dragging the rope, and as they closed in on him the others fell away. By deft maneuvering about the little knot where he was hiding, they let horse after horse escape; and then, as the wild one made his break, Rusty Bill's loop shot out and snapped over his head. Jess dropped his own rope and caught on behind—and the next thing the bronk knew he had stopped breathing. In the frenzy of his madness he skated them across the corral like spiders, but at the first pause they plowed their high-heeled boots into the ground and held fast.

Then, as his eyes began to bulge and his flanks to heave, Rusty Bill walked quietly up the rope, reached out ever so gently and rubbed him on the nose, reached further and touched the noose that was choking off his breath, then with a quick jerk pulled back the *honda* knot and let him breathe. At the second great gasp the wild one recovered his nerve and flew back, wilder than ever, only to be smothered down by the instant tightening of the rope. Once more the horse-tamer loosened the noose and, patting him on the neck, moved the loop up nearer his

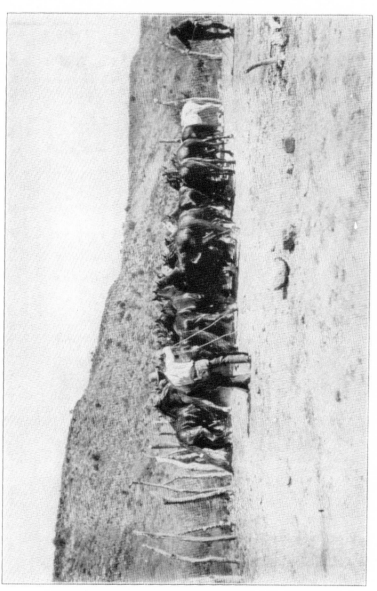

Every Eye is on that Rope, and a Man has to be Quick.

(*Photograph by Dane Coolidge*)

Such Horses Were Never Meant to be Shod.
After kicking aginst the ropes for half an hour, Hoggie sits down to think the matter over.
(*Photograph by Dane Coolidge*)

head. Then he began to pull, very gently, and at the third tug the bronk followed meekly to the gate. His troubles were not over for there were shoes to go on his feet, but he had been initiated into the mystery of the rope.

There was no blacksmith-shop at Blue River —not yet. Every man who took on with the Cherrycow outfit could figure on shoeing his own horses, and on having a choice time doing it. For three days after the horse-cut there was a continuous rumble of feet in the round corral as the cowboys roped out their mounts. Outside the fence, where the shoeing was going on, there was nothing but kicking and cursing and cruelty to animals.

The calmest men became impassioned, the gentlest of them raised their voices to the hills. Ropes were broken, bridle-reins snapped, fence-posts uprooted and bushes trampled flat. Even the horse-tamers flew off the handle and forgot their professional repose before the day was done. Uncle Hal watched the Roman holiday for a minute, sighed and went away. Old Dad, the wagon-boss, lingered around a while in

49

glum disapproval, warned a man or two, and then conveniently absented himself.

Such horses were never intended to be shod, that was the size of it; but the Cherrycow range was one vast rock patch, and no animal could travel over that malpai without shoes. They had to be got on, somehow. At first there was a great uproar as man after man roped his mount and dragged him from the corral, then a general hunting around for shoes and rasps and nails. A cowboy broke into song as he hammered out his cold-wrought shoes, another joined in as he led his horse up and tied him to a post. But when he reached down for its foot the trouble began.

A range horse may tremble like a leaf before his master, but when his feet are touched he is going to kick, strike or bite, generally all three. The cowboys worked in pairs, taking turns at shoeing and holding, and as the struggle progressed every base passion in the human breast rose up against the fighting devil that lurks in a horse. An agent for the S.P.C.A. would have arrested every man on the spot, and then got his head kicked off trying to shoe a front foot.

As for the hind feet, the only way to get them shod was to noose them one at a time in a strong rope, draw them forward and nail the shoes on between kicking spells. When a horse got too bad the boys hog-tied him—threw him down, bound all four feet together, put a pole over his back to hold up the bunch of hoofs and hammered the shoes on regardless. But that strained the muscles of his back and he was never much good for riding. There were a hundred and twenty riding horses driven into the Blue River corral, and every horse came out shod, though he fought like forty devils. It was rough work, and the ground was torn up like a battlefield; but, though the heavens were obscured by the turmoil, there was a greater struggle to come. Every one of those horses had to be rode.

CHAPTER IV

RIDING THEM

IN SHOEING, roping and saddling-up, your Texas cowboy uses all the tricks of the trade; but, once in the saddle, he turns Mr. Outlaw loose. If he wants to put his head down he is welcome; if he wants to hump his back, that is his privilege; and if he wants to buck there is a man in the saddle who will match his proud spirit against anything that wears hair. The Mexicans and Californians use blinds and Spanish bits to check their bucking steeds, but the real thing from Texas mounts them pitching and throws the reins on their neck.

The first man to top off his mount was Outlaw Tom. The corral was still full of horses, waiting to be roped and shod; and when Tom led Scrambled Eggs out into the arena Rusty

53

Bill remarked that he admired his nerve. Not being hired however to give gratuitous advice, the bronco-twisters held the horse until Outlaw Tom got him saddled, then retired to the top of the fence.

Twisting his horse's head to one side Outlaw tried his weight in the stirrup a time or two while Scrambled Eggs sidled warily away. Then, as Tom rose to mount, the shifty sorrel kicked his boot out of the stirrup with a hind foot and ran in among the other horses. The rest was a great cloud of dust, through which horses hurtled by like the wind, a vindictive sorrel cow-kicking at his saddle; and at last, when the frenzied whirly-go-round had ceased, poor Outlaw, limping out of the ruck on one leg. Though things were happening fast, Scrambled Eggs had found time to step on him with both feet, and he was now rollicking round the corral trying to get rid of the rigging. So the bronco-twisters roped him and brought him up to the bars.

"D'ye want me to ride him for you, Tom?" they both inquired at once; but before they

WITH HIS HINDLEG DRAWN UP BY A WELL-ROPE, BLUE DECIDES TO BE A GENTLEMAN.

(*Photograph by Dane Coolidge*)

Not so Scrambled Eggs.

It took both twisters to hold him, while Outlaw Tom tamed him down.

(Photograph by Dane Coolidge)

could get an answer, Bob Greenhouse leapt in and claimed the honor.

"Let *me* ride the so-and-so," he yelled, throwing off the tie-rope. *"I* ain't afraid of the blankety-blank—I can ride him without spurs. Is it a go, Tom? Then turn him loose!"

He grabbed the bridle-reins and a fistful of mane with one hand, caught the horn with the other, and swung up into the saddle. Scrambled Eggs had been wiping things up, so far, and when the Bishop kicked him in the ribs he threw down his head and went to it. In one grand continuation of buck-jumps he charged across the corral, with the fat Bishop rocking back and forth and reaching for the "noodle," while the boys yelled in one high, happy chorus:

"Sta-ay with 'im!"

That is the war-cry of the breaking corral, and the whoops and shouts of laughter that went with it helped to give the occasion a gala hue.

"Stay with the rigging!" they shouted again as the Bishop began to pull leather; and, with one hand on the cantle and the other choking

55

the horn, Bob weathered the storm and rode back in a cloud of glory.

"Gimme a pair of spurs and I'll ride anything in the corral," he announced with a swagger; and Jess Fears took him up.

"All right," he said, snapping off his spurs. "Ride Dan Patch!" But the Bishop waved him away.

"Jest as much obliged," he observed, smiling deprecatingly, "but I guess I've had enough for one day."

Dan Patch was the champion outlaw of the remuda, a large and powerful black, once the top riding-horse of the outfit. The rope was not made that would hold him, nor the man; and when the time before, they had finally got him shod, he had bucked all over the corral with his rigging and finally jumped over the bars. Since then he had been allowed to run loose in the pasture, the leader of the band; but Rusty Bill and Jess Fears had made it up between them to try him another whirl.

This grand climax to the horse-changing drama had been put off till the last day, but

BISHOP GREENHOUSE RIDES SCAMBLED EGGS
WITHOUT SPURS.

(Photograph by Dane Coolidge)

JESS FEARS, THE TWISTER WHO RODE DAN PATCH, ON ANOTHER BRONK.

(Photograph by Dane Coolidge)

when they finally brought him out all hands
quit work to see the battle. Both the twisters had
known Dan Patch in the old days, and they had
a certain affection and respect for him in spite
of his dangerous name; but, in a horse-camp,
sentiment is never allowed to interfere with
business, and when they shook out their ropes
and went after him the black knew just what to
expect.

Crowding in among his fellows, he galloped
round and round the corral, though only their
cold glances and the way they flipped their loops
indicated the interest they took in *him*. There
was a balk or two, a false throw; and then, for
all his dodging, Rusty Bill's rope settled down
over his neck and the fight began. With savage
violence he twitched the rope from Bill's hands
and then, as the end snapped high in the air,
Jess made his throw. That rope was taken from
both of them; other men joined in and lost their
throw-ropes; one of them took a "dally" around
the post and his new grass-rope popped like a
pistol as it broke. A fifth noose settled over his
head, but the powerful bronk dragged five men

57

around the corral until the other horses broke their hold. Then, as he was running free across the corral, poor Dan stepped on the trailing ropes, tripped and fell headlong.

Like a flash Rusty Bill shot through the dust and plumped down on his neck; Jess Fears snatched up the slack of a rope and bound his feet; and there at last, in spite of his struggles, Dan Patch was hog-tied and shod. But, though he was shod, he was not conquered. By main force they had pried up his feet and nailed the iron upon them, but who would swing up on his back and risk his life on the outcome?

"I never see the horse I was afraid of, yet," observed Jess Fears, buckling on his bull-hide leggings, "and I'll ride you, Danny, or know why."

Rusty Bill said nothing, but everybody knew that if Jess failed Bill would follow him. Very gingerly, while his pardner took a "dally" around a post and held the slack, Jess rigged a hackamore or rope halter, and worked it over Dan's ears. There were no signs of fear, only a great caution, a catlike quickness of movement whenever the giant black flicked an ear; and all the time, as Jess edged the blanket up over his shoulder and reached back to Bill for the saddle, he kept up his "breaking patter," the soothing yet derisive talk that horse-tamers use to distract the minds of their mounts.

"No," he said, "you don't look bad to me, Dan Patch! I used to be kind of skeered of ye, but sho, that was all foolishness. He-ere, now, you red-eyed bastard, that'll do! Well, buck then; but I'll git that saddle on you if I have to tie your foot up."

It was not easy to tie Dan Patch's foot up, but up it went at last; and the saddle went on, too. Standing at arm's length Jess tightened up the hind cinch and glanced meaningly at Bill. Then he untied the big rope and lowered Dan's hind foot to the ground. He gathered up the split reins, hooked his toe into the stirrup; and, while all held their breath, slid quietly up into the saddle. There was a moment of intense suspense, a moment when even the Bishop was silent, and all hands waited for the bout that was to come—but Dan Patch did not buck. He stood like a statue, black and still.

"Throw the spurs into him, Jess," suggested

59

Bishop, when the psychological moment had passed; but the bronco-twister only changed his weight in the saddle and waited.

"Spur 'im up—quirt 'im—give 'im the gaff!" clamored the crowd, impatient for the fireworks to begin; but Jess only leaned forward in the saddle and smiled.

"I'm sorry, boys," he said jogging slowly across the corral, "but me and Danny has decided to be friends." And from that day Dan Patch never pitched.

But now the blood of the cowboys was up and they demanded a real victim.

"Why don't you top off old Chalk Eye, Bishop?" inquired a cowboy, when Greenhouse was shouting his loudest.

"I'm afraid to," answered Bob, sarcastically. "Jest been waiting for a *man* to show up! Wouldn't you like to do it for me?"

"Sure thing," retorted the cowboy, "if you'll ride the Fan-tailed Black."

The conversation was rapidly sinking to the level of personalities, without any prospect of bronks being rode, when a little, redheaded,

60

Dan Patch, the Fighting Outlaw, Dragging Five Men by as Many Ropes.
He used to be gentle, till a fool horse-buster spoiled him.

(Photograph by Dane Coolidge)

THE TWO TWISTERS UNDERTAKE TO TAME DANNY.
Jess riggs a hackamore, or rope-halter, and works it over Dan's ears.
(Photograph by Dane Coolidge)

curly-haired man who had just dropped in from
New Mexico, threw away his cigarette and remarked, with a saturnine smile:

"You Arizona fellers seem to have pretty cold
feet, for a hot country."

"How's that?" inquired his neighbors, with
ominous politeness.

"W'y, that Fan-tailed Black don't look so bad
—I thought you Arizona boys could ride."

"Well, you were entiahly misinfo'med, suh,"
observed a hawk-eyed Texan, who had been
watching him ever since he came. "We were jest
waiting for some New Mexico stiff to blow in
and show us how."

"I can't ride for sour beans back home," observed New Mexico, dropping down off the fence
with businesslike directness, "but if you gentlemen will kindly lead that black out into the
rocks, where it will seem a little more natural
for a stranger, I'll do my best to accommodate
you."

He stood aloof as the avid cowboys roped out
the Fan-tailed Black, tied up his foot and cinched
on the center-fire saddle. It was a pretty swell

saddle—everyone admitted that—but the stranger paid no attention to their praise. When the black was saddled and held he picked up his heavy quirt, glanced at his spurs and snapped his leg over the cantle with lightning quickness. Once astride he let out a yell, swung the quirt over his head to give it fire, and lit into the black with both spurs.

Nothing loath, the bronk accepted the challenge, threw a hump into his back, leapt high into the air, turned halfway around and came down stiff-legged—hard. New Mexico's head went back and he grunted, but the moment they hit the ground again he struck both spurs into the Fan-tail's flanks and up they went into the air. In his own way the Fan-tail was as good a fighter as Dan Patch, but New Mexico had made him forget his finesse by that first slash over the rump, and as the quirt continued to descend upon the raw spot he had to break into a run.

Over the rocks and bushes they went, scrambling and pitching, and in the heavy going Fan-tail got so busy keeping on his feet that for the

They Cinch on the Saddle While he is Studying Whether to Kill One of Them or be Good. When Jess mounted him he trotted right off, and never bucked again.

(Photograph by Dane Coolidge)

After Handling Dan Patch Without a Bobble, a Little Job of Horse-Shoeing Looks Easy.

(Photograph by Dane Coolidge)

moment he neglected to buck. Then off came New Mexico's hat. He slapped the black over the head with it and laughed, pinched him in the neck and thumbed him along the shoulders; and as the Fan-tail began once more to "wipe 'er up" in earnest, a belated chorus of Arizona voices rose to the cliffs and over the top of the rimrock:

"Stay with 'im, New Mexico!" they yelled. "Stay with the rigging!" And New Mexico certainly did so.

CHAPTER V

FINDING THE CHERRYCOWS

THE arrival of New Mexico in our midst had given some of the boys a bad scare, as most of them were on the dodge for something; and others, like Sam, were hiding out to keep from killing somebody. One had shot down three men in self-defense and, though acquitted by the jury, had still to consider the surviving relatives, who might be seeking a private revenge. The Reservation at that time was really a sort of hide-out for Texans who had got into trouble; and when, as we were eating dinner, New Mexico and his pardner rode in on us, the cowboys froze like rabbits.

They were both hard-lookers and heavily armed, and every man's first thought was: Officers! The festive note given by two pairs of pink garters dangling gaily from their elbows did not even raise a smile, and Sam was worst scared of all. But, after several minutes of watchful waiting—and in the absence of some more fitting greeter—I rose up and spoke to our guests.

"I'm only a photographer," I said, "taking some pictures of the round-up, but this gentleman here is the cook and if you talk to him right he'll probably give you something to eat."

This broke the ice and, after New Mexico put up such a good ride, the boys finally decided he was all right and took him into the fold. It very soon became known that, far from being officers, these boys were fugitives from justice, having broken up a dance over in New Mexico and set the schoolhouse afire. It was all a mistake and was fixed up later, but there were rewards up for their arrest and they had sworn an oath "never to be took."

On my first arrival at the horse-camp I had run into another man who had stolen a Wine Glass horse and was all set to put up a fight. One of his brothers had been killed while resisting arrest; and another, who had surrendered, was doing a term in the penitentiary; and when he saw me riding down the trail he came out with his six-shooter drawn. But as I started down the steep dip my pack slipped; and, before I got into camp, it slipped again.

Now this is not the way that deputy sheriffs' packs act, especially when they are looking for trouble; and he had a chance to satisfy himself that I was not an officer of the law. From past experience I had learned never to carry a gun, and he finally decided I was harmless. But at the same time he was very uneasy and, much to the relief of the horse-camp man, he saddled up and left.

This made me doubly welcome with Uncle Hal and, as I had some malted milk tablets which he could dissolve and use on his mush, he did me the honor of listening while I told the story of my trip in. A cowboy on Salt River in the Four Peaks country had started me on my quest, and I had staged into Globe from Phoenix with a letter from the sheriff. It was addressed to Rimrock Thompson, the sheriff of Gila County, whom I found in his office of a Saturday night, surrounded by old cronies and friends. But Mr. Thompson, while welcoming me to his county, was quite unable to locate the Cherrycows, who were out on the Reservation somewhere and might not be back for a month.

He submitted my problem to the assembled old-timers who informed me that the country was entirely uninhabited and I would save myself a lot of trouble by turning around and going home. I was spared that ignominy however by a slightly intoxicated gentleman who dropped in. He had seen a bunch of them at Bylas that morning, and they were going down to Safford to bring up a band of horses. So all I had to do was to take the morning train down and I could catch them at Bylas, coming back.

This sounded easy, but when I got to Bylas, with my camera and bed-roll, there was not a soul in sight. Nothing but the shipping-pens and a vacant house in the distance; and from the brush along the river I could hear the Apaches singing.

In order to turn me back the sheriff had told me the sad fate of two other ambitious young photographers, who had gone out on the Reservation in a quest for Cherrycow pictures. One had got thrown off his horse and broken an arm and the other had been caught in a month-long storm, which had spoiled all his hard-won films and soaked his camera to pieces. I was sitting up on the corral searching the horizon for dust and wondering if discretion is the better part of valor when, out from behind the brush, there emerged a hobo who asked me for something to eat. That, unfortunately, was something I did not have, but I gave him a dollar to bounce on when he said he could buy food from the Mexican section hands.

He was a desperate-looking character and had a hard-luck story a mile long, which he had to get out of his system before he could go. For an hour or more he sat beside me on the fence and I had about decided that his intentions leaned towards highway robbery when we spied a dust in the south. It was the Cherrycow horse-herd being hazed up the river, and changed the situation entirely. I was about to leave with these friends, I told him, and then the truth came

69

out. What he was waiting for was to ask me if I could give him the dollar in dimes and quarters, as the Mexicans never had any change. They would feed him for nothing, as far as that went, but he preferred to pay for his grub; and the first *paisano* who gave him the tortillas and beans would get the whole dollar, leaving him broke.

That was a reasonable explanation and, as my cowboy friends were approaching, I made bold to take the dollar back before I gave him the change. He drifted off up the track as the Cherrycow boys came in sight, and they told me to go back to San Carlos and join the outfit from there. They were just passing through and I could not keep up with them, even if I had a horse, so I took their good advice and waited at San Carlos for three days, for someone to guide me out. But everybody was quitting and nobody was going back, so I hired a pinto pony and struck out by myself.

The pony got stuck in the quicksand when we came to the crossing of the Gila, and by the time I had dug him out the morning was well advanced. But we were following a wide trail, and every cowboy who came in had told me how to find the camp. They failed to agree in several important particulars but all said I couldn't get lost, as the road was always within sight of the old military telegraph line, which would take me right to the Garden, a short day's journey from San Carlos.

This Garden was an oasis in the middle of the Reservation, where a Mexican raised vegetables for the cowboys and guarded their surplus supplies. Just follow the telegraph line, they said, and you can't possibly go wrong—yet everyone of them seemed to have got lost. I was told afterward by the cook that one new cowboy had come into camp three times the first morning in the belief that he was somewhere else, taking part in the round-up.

The country was very deceiving, looking level as a floor for miles, yet breaking off into narrow, unseen chasms, cut down into the malpai plain. A road across these mesas looked like a double stone-wall, where they had thrown out rocks on both sides; and they had finally given the roads up and gone back to trails and pack-trains. Several times I was in danger of getting lost, but the sight of the telegraph line, constructed of hollow iron poles, always put me on my course. Along the way I came upon mysterious bundles of grass and crossed sticks, left by wandering Apaches for the information of their friends. But to a white man these signs meant nothing, and the Indians kept out of sight. They were probably killing cattle and jerking the meat while they watched me from afar.

Towards sundown my horse gave out, being loaded with all my photographic plates and my bed, but I kept on for a couple of hours after dark, leading him. I had hoped to reach Warm Springs, where there was water, but had to make a dry camp. In the morning I could see the telegraph line extending before me for at least fifty miles across a perfectly level plain. And yet all the cowboys had told me I could get to the Garden in one day. Just follow the telegraph line!

But the longer I looked at that row of poles the more I felt that something was wrong. It was simply impossible to hide any garden in the midst of that lava-strewn plain. At last I drew a quarter from my pocket and tossed it into the air.

"Heads I go ahead," I said. "Tails I turn back."

It came tails and I was glad. Once more I had got caught out without adequate food—I had just enough to last me back to Carlos—and on going back a mile I found a water-hole which I had passed in the dark. There was a bunch of cattle there, sipping up the fouled seep; and, walking around among them, a young wolf. I knew he was a wolf by his big ears and short tail, but he came up to me like a dog. Probably never in his life had he seen a man on foot, but he had a bad look in his eye and I drove him away with rocks.

The pony filled up with water and began eating grass. He was a lazy little rascal, as fat as butter, and had not lost a pound from his long journey, although he was getting footsore. So I decided to walk, letting him carry the pack, and we had just got lined out for San Carlos when,

73

on the edge of a deep canyon, I came across another telegraph line. It ran straight up the side of a cactus-covered mountain, heading north, and disappeared over the top, and I was satisfied it went to the Garden. But if I climbed up that rocky hill with my tender-footed pony and it *didn't,* it would mean two days back to town.

I had passed under this branch wire in the night-time, and the cowboys must have forgotten about it. Or had they?

There was no use trying to reason it out from what I had been told when everybody in the country got lost, so I left it to luck and flipped the quarter again. It came tails—go back. But there was something about that line of poles, leading so resolutely up the high ridge, that indicated an ultimate purpose. It was going somewhere.

"Make it the best two out of three," I said. And it came heads—twice.

So we climbed up the black mountain, whose loose lava hurt my pony's sore feet; and from the summit I gazed down upon a broad strip of green—cottonwoods, a creek, and a Garden. *The*

74

"New Mexico" Shows the Texans How to Ride.

(Photograph by Dane Coolidge)

DINNER ON THE OPEN RANGE.

(*Photograph by Dane Coolidge*)

Garden! If I had followed the main line of telegraph poles I would have come out over in New
Mexico somewhere. The cowboys had all forgotten about this fork in the wire, but now I
knew I was on the right trail. It was a long trip
for Pinto down the other side of that mountain
but, after a drink of clear water, we fell into a
good trail and headed up the canyon. If I had
known about this trail before I started I could
have saved sorefooting my horse, but I ate a few
milk tablets, which made me hungrier than
ever, and kept on towards the Garden.

It was only a small patch of ground, planted
mostly to cabbages, and as I approached the gate
I saw, up on the hillside, a Mexican and a dog.
Neither moved and I went inside, and pretty
soon old Manuel came down. He had lived
there so long he was spooky about strangers,
but when he found I could speak a little Spanish he got friendly and fed me some beans.
Then he began to talk, and I listened for two
days. Half the time I didn't know what he was
talking about, but there was a great deal about
a big black snake down in Sonora that had a

golden cross on its head. It lived in a cave on the mountain and the people offered it milk and young chickens and worshiped it like a god.

Manuel was camped under a tree but he had a house there and every once in a while I would hear the loud ringing of a telephone, to which he paid no attention whatever. On the second day, while he was off down the canyon, I ventured to answer this call and a big, Texas voice jumped out at me. He was trying to speak Spanish and when I answered in English he burst into wholehearted curses. But at the same time he was glad. For a week or more the boys north of Black River had been trying to get the Garden. They were out of grub and everything else, but Manuel had never answered the phone. They thought he had gone crazy or run away, and told me, when he came back, to tell the so-and-so to *answer,* by grab, or they would kill him.

Manuel came in after a while and, very reluctantly, listened to the phone. But to him it was a magical and awesome instrument and he hung up after a few words. Then I took it down and got the news. The outfit was due at Black River in two days. I could go on to the horse-camp at Blue River, and Uncle Hal would show me the trail to the ferry. But tell that blank-blanked Mexican to send up some grub or they would work him over good.

I told Manuel just that, as he had been keeping me there for two days in order to have some-one to talk to, but he said that some Apaches were watching his camp, and if he left they would steal all the supplies. It was better that he should stay there until the cow*boys* came in, but he would make me a picture of the trail in the dust and perhaps I could find my way. He was more than a little *loco* and spent most of his daytime watching the trail, up which nobody ever came; but at night he went crazy over a dollar watch, which he was trying to make keep time.

It had to be hung up by a string or it would not run at all. He could wind it from behind, like a clock, but the part that moved the hands was broken off. So the only thing to do, as he had doped it out, was to wait until my watch and his registered the same—*then* wind his up and presto it would keep good time! Repeatedly during that last night this crazy Mexican woke me up to ask what time it was, and I pulled out early the next morning, before he went clear off his head.

He drew me an elaborate picture in the dust, of the trail and all the landmarks; and tagged along over the rim, to see that I took the right turn. But, shortly after leaving him, I came across two shod-horse tracks leading north through a flat covered with lava; and as he had spoken of two cowboys who had passed through on their way to the horse-camp, I decided to trail them in. But hardly had I turned off from the prescribed way than Manuel, who had been hiding, rose up from behind a rock and began to shout and wave his arms.

I had taken quite a little from this *paisano* already and when, in his flow of invective, I recognized several cuss-words I told him where to go in two languages. Then I picked up the tracks of those two cowboys and trailed them in

to the horse-camp. There, except for my run-in
with the horse-thief who thought I was an officer of the law, I was given a very cordial welcome; and Uncle Hal told me that old Manuel
could speak English as well as I could. He had
just said he couldn't to make me talk Spanish—
but anyhow, he knew what I thought of him.

Mr. Young laughed heartily at my experi-
ences, which he said were the usual thing; and
that afternoon the new cook dragged in, after
trailing the cowboys for a week. Words could
hardly express Mr. Elkins' indignation at an
outfit that would send in for a cook and then
leave their raft on the wrong side of the river,
expecting him to swim across. It took time, but
after he got it off his chest he felt better; and
the next day, with Uncle Hal to guide us, we
rode in to Black River Crossing in the best of
health and spirits. For a tenderfoot I had done
pretty well, having been lost only five days
while he had been out eight. Not lost, of course
—he knew where he was—just trying to find the
outfit.

IN THE EARLY MORNING COLD,
even the gentle mounts were mean and had to be uncocked.
(Photograph by Dane Coolidge)

CHAPTER VI

THE ROUND-UP

Now we were back at the horse-camp, with fresh mounts and full packs, and the Cherrycow boys prepared once more to round up cattle, cut out the cows and calves, brand and move on, until the spring was gone. The first day out we would camp at Warm Springs, where the cattle came in by the thousand to drink the tepid water; and the cowboys crawled into bed early, for there would be work enough in the morning. No, they did not wrap themselves in a single blanket and, with their saddle for a pillow, fall into a dreamless sleep. That is all right for poetry and cowboy songs, but saddles make very poor pillows and the Cherrycow men had to sleep.

They did not spend a third of their lives in

81

bed, by any means; but that, as one of them remarked, snuggling down under two pairs of
army blankets, was all the more reason for sleeping well. Those who did not sport mattresses
had folding cots, with two extra comforts for
padding. Every man in the outfit had a "tarp"
of heavy canvas, eighteen feet long by eight feet
wide; and most of them had tents, too, for a
cowboy has to lie out in all kinds of weather and
his bed is all the home he has.

They would not even throw in with each
other, but each man had his separate bed, and
it took a good horse to carry it. Only in the matter of his pillow was the cowboy still economical
—it was the same old war-bag, made out of ticking
and stuffed with his entire wardrobe, his cigarette papers and all his worldly goods. With his
head on that he sank into a brief sleep, soon
to be broken by the rough hand of some pardner, rousing him to stand his guard—or the
shouts of that human alarm-clock, the cook. On
account of the grass being fed off near the water
it was necessary to hold the horses a mile or
more from camp and, ten minutes after his yell,

the night guard came tearing in over the rocks, leaving the herd for the Indian horse-wrangler to pick up.

By that time the lucky boys who had not been selected to stand guard had rolled out of their sumptuous beds, stamped on their boots, washed up, and then religiously wiped their faces on a dirty towel kept for that purpose. As the cook swung the ponderous covers off his ovens there was a general scramble for cups and plates; and when he said, "Go to it!" they responded to a man. In one deep oven there was beef, cut in slices and fried in grease. The other contained sour-dough biscuits, white and regular, and there was coffee in the pot; but every man made a point for the mush-kettle.

Can after can of evaporated milk was punctured and thrown away empty, the sugar-sack stood open with a cup in it; but not until the kettle was scraped clean would the childlike cowboys give up their lick and sweetness and go back to "good hard grub."

It was still dark when the clatter of stones announced the arrival of the horse-herd; but the boss immediately got up, placed his plate and cup in the dishpan, and said:

"Well, boys, hurry up now and catch your hawses!"

The day's work had begun.

In the horse-changing every man had drawn two gentle horses and three bronks, but in the cold chill of early dawn even the gentle mounts were mean and wild. At sight of a saddle-blanket they flew back twenty feet, and every time a saddle was swung up on a wild one he bucked it off and kicked at it. Here once more was a situation which none of the Christian virtues would solve, and soon the canyon was filled with the sound of cursing and scuffling as man after man relapsed into savagery and fought it out among the rocks.

When, with the assistance of the twisters, the wild ones were all saddled up, the topping off began. Those who had gentle horses mounted first, to keep the bronks out of the thorny mesquite-trees and hackberries; and then, as cowboy after cowboy crawled his pitching mount and went plunging off over the water-worn

84

boulders, the cliffs echoed to whoops and shouts and peals of boisterous laughter, growing fainter and fainter as the outfit dashed away and spread out for the morning's gather.

In little parties of three and four the round-up hands rode off, each heading through some draw or saddle for its particular station. The silence of the wilderness settled once more over the camp and the lava plain that lay above it, dotted with herds of grazing cattle. Then suddenly a dark line appeared in the distance—a line that wavered and changed with the rush of horsemen behind it—and all the near-by cattle stopped grazing and raised their heads to listen. Clear and shrill yet pinched to an insect-like faintness, came the high-keyed whoops of the cowboys, and as the line drew nearer the syllables of their yelling became plain.

"*Aye—aye—aye! Yeeee—pah! Ah-hah-hah-hah!*"

The Texans learned those yells from the bloodthirsty Comanches, so they say, and there is certainly something barbarous about them, rising like the cry of prairie wolves above the bawling of cows and calves and the thunderous roar of bulls.

As the line advanced toward the cutting-grounds every dark canyon along the way belched forth its quota of flying steers, followed by cowboys on nimble steeds that skated over the rocks like lizards. With tumultuous and mournful cries they drifted down towards the open space in front of the big corral; and there in a mighty chorus they bellowed out their protests, while mothers sought out their calves and bulls plowed sullenly through the herd.

According to range law no calf can be branded unless it is with its mother, and, as many of them had become separated in the drive, it was necessary to let them get together again before the cutting began. While these reunions were being consummated the cowboys jogged over to the branding corral—into which George, the Apache wrangler, had already driven the remuda—to change mounts.

The Cherrycow outfit always had an Indian for a horse-wrangler. The boys said it was because no white man would take the job—but

George, the Apache Horse-Wrangler, Brings in the "Remuda," singing *Hee, hee-yah; hee, hee-yah; heeeee!* as if he were king of all that land.

(Photograph by Dane Coolidge)

THE TWISTER TOPS OFF A BAD ONE.

(*Photograph by Dane Coolidge*)

George seemed to think it was "all right." That
was a favorite word with him; and they kept
him using it, too. When he wasn't hunting
horses or grazing the remuda along some draw,
he was dragging up wood for the cook or doing
a little job of shoeing. Four hours' sleep was
about all he could count on, as he went out with
the herd every night, yet as soon as they woke
him up he would begin to sing Indian songs;
and all day, as he sat on some butte with his
horses feeding below, he would tap two sticks
together and chant: *"Hee, hee-yah; hee, hee-
yah; heeee!"* as if he were the king of all that
land.

The midday changing of mounts was generally the occasion for an outbreak on the part of
the bronks. In the early morning the cowboys
were afraid to tackle their bronco horses, but in
the heat of noonday their courage rose and man
after man caught up a wild one. In case any of
them refused to pitch, the puncher threw the
spurs into him and slapped him over the head
with his hat—and, after the dust had settled, the
horse was considered to be officially uncocked.

This pleasing ceremony being over, and the cattle by that time settled down, the boys returned to begin cutting, while George took the remuda out to fill them up with grass.

Cutting is the one job where the Texans feel repressed. It has to be done quietly. No whooping, no rough-riding, no fancy swearing goes. The wagon-boss and three or four of the steadiest hands ride slowly about through the immense herd of cattle until they have identified the mothers of most of the calves. Then, being careful to keep them together, they work the cows and calves out to the edge and stampede them across the open to a hold-up herd.

With a big herd they cut from both sides at once, the remainder of the outfit being kept busy holding the cattle and turning back strays. It was a tedious process but, two hours after the work began, every calf with a bona-fide mother had been cut out and the main herd turned loose to drift back to its accustomed grounds. Then the bawling cows and calves were thrown into the strong branding corral, while the outfit raced to camp for dinner.

Branding is a brutal job, at best; but it only happens once, and with the Cherrycows it happens quick. They use the Texas method—which is much faster than the tie-down Mexican style, though it takes more men. When the battery of stamp-irons has been heated red hot over the long fire, two cowboys, with their throw-ropes tied short to the horn, ride out into the herd, get a calf to stepping, and noose him by the hind foot. He is then dragged up to the fire, where a flanker grabs him across the shoulders by the hide, boosts him off the ground with his knees and slams him to mother earth.

Instantly another man seizes him by the upper hind foot, sits down behind him and places his boot against the lower hind leg, meanwhile throwing loose the rope. The poor calf is no sooner held than two cheery gentlemen begin to burn Cs on him, while another works over his ears with a sharp knife. There is a cloud of white smoke, an agonizing bawl, and all is over. The calf has a large C on his jaw, and a larger one still on his shoulder and hip. His left ear is notched to a swallow-fork, and his right ear sharped to a point. He is a little dogie now and will be a beef-steer by-and-by.

The ear-marker puts the keys from the swallow-forks in his hip pocket as he proceeds and, when the branding is over, the boss counts them solemnly in the fence corner, writing down the tally in his book. Then the cows and calves are turned loose and the outfit lopes back to camp, thirsty and tired and grimed to the ears with dirt.

There was a great race to water that first "evening" and as soon as the cowboys had got a drink and turned their horses into the corral, half of them lopped down and fell asleep before Sam could holler for supper. It is hard work, punching cows. But, after eating, some of the daintiest, after going through their war-bags for clean clothes, went down to the nice warm spring and took a bath. The first one in a month maybe, and after it was over there was a layer of brand-new underclothes thrown away along the bank.

It was easier to buy new ones in town than to go to the trouble of washing them: and the

Apache squaws, when they saw a cowboy coming, ran for the rocks like mad. There was no use hollering to them and holding up the dirty clothes. They had a fixed opinion of cowboys which no amount of wheedling could change, and George only shook his head. There had been trouble between his people and the Cherrycows, and he wanted to hold his job.

The next morning a band of Apache bucks rode into camp, waiting hopefully for the cowboys to get through eating, in case there might be something left. But Sam, when the outfit had gone, deliberately threw the food into the dirt. His opinion of Apaches could be expressed without words, and when they tried to talk to the boss he pretended not to understand. They had lost a steer, or had it branded by the Cherrycows, but the way they mixed their words up it was no wonder old Dad was confused.

"Morton say—this feller—belongs to him—that steer," was the best George could do at interpreting; and if the Indians got any beef they had to steal it, as usual. With them, stealing had always been a virtue—they only punished their children when they got caught. Their method of getting beef as outlined by the station-men, was as follows: They would go to the agent and get a permit to gather mescal, a kind of yucca with a very sweet heart. Then the bucks would send the women ahead to hack out the yucca heads and throw them into a pit with a lot of hot rocks, where they would let them roast for three days.

When all the heavy work had been done and it was time to open the pit the men would ride out to help the squaws eat it and maybe brew up a little *tulapai,* their favorite drink. This leaves them pleasantly intoxicated without ruining their dispositions like whiskey; and if they happen to get a little fresh beef the expedition is considered a success. The roasted mescal heads are very good eating, but the fibers will take the skin off a white man's tongue before he has consumed very much. The *tulapai* is made from fermented corn, flavored with tobacco smoke, and makes them dance and sing; and to that they like to add a young Company beef, newly killed and broiled over the coals.

At the mouth of some box canyon, scouts would be posted, to watch for any chance cowboy. Then the yearling would be roped and led up to the mescal pits, where it would be killed and the hide carefully hid. The appearance of some station-man would be signaled by puffs of smoke, and by the time he got up to the pits all the Indians would be eating mescal. The year before, a young man from Texas had crowded the Indians too close and they had shot at him from the rocks, but he had ridden in and routed them with his six-shooter.

The truth is the Apaches had refrained from killing him for fear their permits would be cut off, but they placed their bullets very close. Jesse Fears and his pardner had been in the White Mountains all winter, standing off the warriors from Fort Apache; but the northern Indians had butchered so many cows that Henry Boice was moving them away. There was bad blood on both sides, and all the old hands carried saddle-guns, but the Indians did not dare kill them. It would interfere with their jerked-beef industry.

The day after they got their horses shod and went back to their regular work the Cherry-cow boys began to sing and tell jokes. The constant fight with bad horses had sapped even their rugged strength, but as the cool night wind sucked up the ravine they gathered about the fire, moving closer as the coals died down, and told stories of the only world they knew. Stories of the old-time drives from Texas to Wyoming and Montana; of romantic adventures in Chihuahua and Mexico; of long, wintry rides on the chuck-line, when all the ranches were full-handed and no one would take on a poor cowboy; of fierce brawls in frontier towns and the glories of the Fourth in Globe.

Painted in the gaudy colors of their vernacular, the cowboy life took on the halo of a great adventure, and the gloomiest of them were warming to the theme when the gaunt shadow of the wagon-boss fell upon them and broke the spell of their dreams.

"Well, boys," he said, "you'd better take the hawses out now—it's nigh on to a mile to any feed. John, you and Jess stand the first guard;

THE DAY'S WORK BEGINS—CUTTING THE HERD.

(*Photograph by Dane Coolidge*)

THERE IS A CLOUD OF WHITE SMOKE, A SINGLE AGONIZING BAWL, AND ALL IS OVER.

(Photograph by Dane Coolidge)

Tom and Bishop the second; George and Kinch third, Lee and Albert fourth. Take your beds with you, and start 'em towards camp as soon as you can see light—we're working Black Mesa in the mawning."

BRANDING, TEXAS FASHION.

At the right, the battery of irons is on the fire. While two men hold a calf a third brands him with three Cs—one on the jaw, one on the ribs and one on the hip—while a fourth man marks the ears.

(Photograph by Dane Coolidge)

STANDING GUARD.

(Photograph by Dane Coolidge)

CHAPTER VII

COWBOY SONGS AND STORIES

AT LAST we were back to the cowboy's normal life, with cattle to round up and guards to stand and time to sing and joke. Being on the upper range, the cows were turned loose every night; but the horses had to be close-herded or they would slip away and escape. Two at a time, the boys stood night-guard, four guards of two and a half hours apiece, beginning at seven P.M.; and, after a hard day's work, the principal part of the job was keeping awake. If they ever got to dozing or "sleeping on their hand" there would be some horses lost, so the night-herders began to sing.

Perhaps, in handling cattle, the words of the old song are true:

> What keeps the herd from running,
> Stampeding far and wide?
> The cowboy's long, low whistle
> And singing by their side.

97

But the Cherrycow boys were trying to keep *themselves* awake, and they began by singing endless songs. A song that was short was no good to them, and the best-loved were regular ballads. They could improvise on these—no two versions the same—and they never let it worry them if one line was a little too long or short, or some stanza had a couple of extra lines. If you ever see a cowboy song that is correct in rhyme and rhythm, the chances are it has been worked over by some technically educated collector.

I was collecting songs myself, but I wanted them the way they came, spelling and all. Many old English words would crop up in the texts, but as long as I could understand them I let them go—and I made the cowboys write them down themselves. The first man I edged in on was Outlaw Tom, who had got bucked off again. He was lying in the shade at Warm Springs and, while he nursed his numerous wounds which he had got on top of some old ones when his horse fell among the rocks, he was singing a dolorous tune. I made a trade with him—three pictures for the words of one song—after which he went on to discuss his extraordinary run of hard luck.

"Yes, sir," he said, "I done lost my nerve, and the hawses all seem to know it. When I was breaking bronks at Safford I could ride anything that wore hair. I wasn't afraid of nothing, until I stepped up on old Quinine and he throwed me and broke my shoulder. Eight days later we had a riding contest and I drawed old Quinine again; but my shoulder hadn't healed. I was afraid I'd hurt it, and I got bucked off twice. The third time he wouldn't pitch, but my nerve was gone, and I couldn't ride for sour apples.

"I quit busting bronks then and took on with the Cherrycows, where the work wouldn't be quite so hard; but the first week out I got all skinned up, when one of them throwed me down hill among the rocks. I was just getting healed up when a gentle old hawse I was riding fell down and skinned me all over again, and it's been like that ever since. I'm like that cowboy in the song, that tried to ride the gol-darned wheel. I'm busted, from my sombre to my heel.

"No, I don't know the words to that song, but Jess Fears can give them to you. *He* ain't skeered of nothing, but wait till he's had a few falls. I've been trying to git my nerve back—I'll ride anything and fight anybody—but I've had a long run of bad luck. After I quit at Safford I went up to St. Johns, a Mormon town in Apache County. Got fined three times my first three trips, and when I went in on the Fourth of July I resolved to keep out of all fights. I stayed away from the saloons and the tough part of town, until I got to hating myself so bad I decided to go home.

"On my way down the street I met a feller that felt the same as I did. He said they were all a bunch of so-and-sos, and he could lick any this-and-that in town. He was a big, strapping feller but I asked him if that included me, and he said it did. So I tied into him and it cost me fifty dollars, beside a doctor's bill of twenty-five dollars more for the other feller's eyes. They were leading him around by a string when I left.

"This St. Johns was a fighting burg. On one side of the street it was all Mormons and on the other side all Mexicans; two kinds of people I don't like. So I went on to Flagstaff, where they

100

were mostly lumberjacks and Swedes. I was looking for a job but I couldn't find one; but I kept out of trouble for two weeks, being drunk most of the time. My head wasn't working quite right—I was still looking for trouble—and when I asked one of two men to have a drink with me and the other feller came up too, I knocked his glass off the bar. Then I asked him what he meant, trying to drink with a gentleman, and he beat hell out of me.

"I was going down the street, staggering along the sidewalk, when I met another drunk, and *he* was staggering. When I turned to the right I ran into him; and when I turned to the left, he was there. I tried to make him turn to the right, like he ought to, and he whipped me again. Before I could get out of town I ran into another feller and *he* whipped me, too. I got licked three times in fifteen minutes, and went into a dance-hall for a drink. But when the women saw my cowboy boots they screamed and told me to keep out.

"It seems they had a big lumberjack in behind there and the girls were all entertaining

101

him so he wouldn't start a fight; but do you think that turned me back? No, sir, I might be losing my nerve but I wouldn't be bluffed by no lumberjack.

" 'Just the man I'm looking for!' I hollered. 'Show me the so-and-so!'

"And believe it or not, when I went in after him, that big Swede got up and left!"

Tom was a mild-looking man, but as limber and tough as a rawhide reata and with the proper fighting spirit. He might be down, but he was far from being out; and, while he was waiting for his wounds to heal, he wrote down the words of that song.

MY FRIENDS AND RELATIONS

My friends and relations has caused a separation
Concerning the part of some favorite one
Besides their vexation and great troubblation
They will sometime be sorry
        for what they have done.

My fortune is small, I will truly confess it
But what I have got it is all of my own

I might have lived long in the
　　world and enjoyed it
If my cruel friends could have left me alone.

Farewell to this country, I now must leave it
And seek my way to some far distant land
My horse and my saddle is a
　　source of all pleasures
And when I meet friend I'll join hart and hand.

For gold it is said to be a source of all evil,
And beauty a thing that the ladies adore.
I've got money a-plenty to bear all expenses
And when it is gone I know how to git more.

Farewell to the girl that I no more shall see
This world is wide and I'll spend it in pleasures.
I don't care for no girl that Don't care for me
I'll drink and be jolley and not
　　care for no downfall.

I'll drown my troubles in a bottle of wine
I'll drown them away in a full flowing bowl.
And ride through the wild to pass away time
And when Death calls for me
　　I'll follow him home.

I'll be honest and fare in all my transactions
Whatever I do I intend to be true.

Here is health and good wishes
to all you fair ladys
It is hard, boys, to find one
that will always be true.

This is a typical cowboy song of the senti-
mental kind and it was not long before I had
Jess Fears working nights to write down a funny
one.

THAT GOL DARN WHEEL

I can take the wildest bronco
of the wild and woolly west
I can back him, I can ride him,
let him do his level best.
I can handle any creature
ever wore a coat of hair
And I had a lively tussle
with a tarnal grizzley bear.

I can rope and tie a longhorn
of the wildest Texas brand
And in any disagreement
I can play a leading hand.
But at last I met my master
and I shortly had to squeal

104

When the boys got me astraddle
    of that gol darn wheel.

It was at the Eagle Rancho
    on the Brazos where I first ran across
The dang contrivance
    that upset me in the dust.
It naturally up and throwed me,
    it stood me on my cussed head,
And it tramped my face in lightning order,
    so the foreman said.

It was a tenderfoot that brought it,
    he was wheeling away
From the home of freedom
    out to San Francisco Bay.
He tied it up at the Rancho
    to get outside of a meal
Never thinking that us cowboys
    would monkey with the wheel.

There was old Arizona Jim McGinty,
    all the same as Jack McGill,
Who said there was a man who broke
    the limit a bragging on his riding skill
A puncher not a million miles away
    who thought himself a rider,
Well, he is tolerable gay.

And there came an intermission,
    this same fellow as he meant
Is a mighty handy critter
    as far as horses went,
But he would find he was bucking
    agin a different sort of deal
When he pops his leather leggings
    across the gol darn wheel.

Such a slur upon my talent
    made me hotter than a mink
I told them I could ride it,
    for amusement or for chink.
As it was only a plaything
    for the boys to have in their mount
I would have their idol shattered
    when they trot the critter out.

The grade was kinda sloping
    from the Rancho to the creek
We went a galapalocking
    like a crazy lightning streak.
A whizzing and a buzzing,
    first to this side and then to that
The contrivance kinda wobbled
    like the flying of a bat.

You could hear those punchers yelling:
    "Stay with her, Uncle Bill!
Hit her with your spurs, you sucker.
    Turn her muzzle up the hill!"
NO, I never paid no attention;
    no, I never looked around
For my eyes were kept quite busy
    looking for the smoothest ground.

And a kind of sneaking idea
    through my head began to steal
That the devil had a mortgage
    on the gol darn wheel.
I began to comprehend as down the hill I went
There is going to be a smash-up
    that I can't circumvent.

I have a dim and hazy recollection of the stop
Of the world all spinning around
    and the stars all tangled up.
When at last I found I was at the rancho
    with those cowboys gathered around
And the medico was sewing
    on the hide where it had ripped.

And old Arizona says: "Well, old boy,
    I guess you're whipped."

I told him I was busted
    from my sombre to my heel.
He sorta grinned and said:
    "That's nothing.
You oughter see the gol darn wheel."

This was hot stuff and the boys all wanted a copy of it. They were like a lot of housewives exchanging recipes, only a cowboy hates to write. They would rather work all day for the price of three pictures than dash off a little song; but that was my price and I stuck to it. If they didn't know any songs themselves they could get them from somebody else; and it made no difference if they couldn't spell. The next song I got was from Cherrycow Charley, the man who had been our makeshift cook; and it had so much of the old-time color, that I had to cut off the last three stanzas.

BALLAD OF RUTE HOG OR DIE

I am a Jolly Cowboy I Hunt all the time
I can whip the sonofawhich
    that stole a cow of mine

I'll climb up on his Hocks
  you bet your life I'll try
Comb His Head With A Six Shuter
  Rute Hog or die.

Out on the plaines Site to be seen
Antelopes and Dear and the grass growen green
The mustang gang and the indian crye
Ride around the cattle Boys
Rute Hog or die.

Out in camp I tell you What they eat
A peace of cold Bread and a peace of cold meat
A little black coffee and Whiskey on the sly
Ride around the cattle Boys
Rute Hog or die.

Out in camp nothing for to do
Damned old cow horses for to shoe
Throw your rope around them,
    down you make them lie
Ride around the cattle Boys,
Rute Hog or die.

I got more like that, and some worse; but Jess
saved the honor of the Lone Star State by giving
me an old version of "The Dying Ranger."

With Texas cowboys this song is a paean of grief—they want to cry when they sing it—and it expresses as no other their passionate love of country and loyalty to a friend.

THE DYING RANGER

The summer sun was setting
    and fell with a lingering ray
Thru the branches of a forest
    where a wounded ranger lay.
In the shade of a fair palmetto,
    'neath the summer's sultry sky
Far away from his loved old Texas
    they have laid him down to die.

A group had gathered round him,
    companions in the fight,
The tears poured down each manly cheek
    as he bade his last goodnight.
One true friend and companion
    was kneeling by his side
Trying to quench his life-blood flowing;
    but alas, in vain he tried.

When in despair and anguish
    he saw it was in vain

While down this loved companion's cheek
    the tears poured down like rain
Up spoke this dying ranger, saying:
    "Do not weep for me!
"I am crossing the dark, dark river,
    to a country that is free.

"Draw nearer to me, comrades,
    and listen to what I say;
"I am going to tell a story
    as my spirit hastes away;
"Way down in Northeast Texas,
    that good old 'Lone-Star State'
"There is one who for my coming
    with an anxious heart will wait.

"A little girl, my sister,
    my only joy and pride,
"I've loved her since her childhood
    for I've had no one beside.
"I've loved her as a brother
    and with a brother's care,
"I have tried through grief and sorrow
    her little heart to cheer.

"Our country was invaded,
    they called for volunteers;

"She threw her arms around my neck
    and bursting into tears,
"Saying, 'Go, my darling brother,
    drive the traitors from our shore,
"My heart may need your presence,
    but our country needs you more.'

" 'Tis true I love my country,
    to it I've given my all;
"If it was not for my sister, boys,
    I'd be content to fall.
"Oh comrades, I am dying,
    she'll never see me more,
"Tho' she'll vainly wait my coming
    at our little cottage door."

"My mother, she lies sleeping
    beneath the churchyard's sod,
" 'Tis many a long and weary year
    since her spirit went to God.
"My father, he lies sleeping
    beneath the dark blue sea;
"We have no other kindred,
    there is only Nell and me.

"Draw nearer to me, comrades,
    and listen to my dying prayer;

"Who'll be to her a brother,
    and protect her with his care?"
Up spoke those noble rangers
    in a chorus, one and all:
"We will be to her a brother
    till the strongest of us fall."

One happy smile of pleasure
    o'er the ranger's face was spread
One quickened pulse and shudder,
    and the ranger boy was dead.
On the banks of the Brazos river
    they have laid him down to rest
With his saddle for a pillow
    and the Lone Star on his breast.

CHAPTER VIII

HERD SONGS AND BALLADS

IT TAKES time to sing a ballad but a cowboy standing guard has lots of it, and it is during the long watches of the night that they learn each other's songs. Many old folk-songs, brought over from England, are passed along in this way; and one of the most beautiful of them dates back to Dick Turpin, the highwayman. He was hung in 1739 for horse-stealing; but his love for Bonnie Black Bess, put into song, has endured for nearly two centuries. Sam White, from Toyah, Texas, learned this song from his folks.

BONNIE BLACK BESS

When Fortune, blind goddess,
Fled my abode
Kind friends proved unfaithful
So I took to the road

To plunder the wealthy
To relieve my distress,
I bought you to aid me
My Bonnie Black Bess.

No vile whip or spurs
Did thy sides ever gall
Nor did you need them,
You would bound at my call.
For each act of kindness
You would me caress,
You are never unfaithful
My Bonnie Black Bess.

When dark, sable midnight
Her mantle had thrown
O'er the bright face of Nature
Many times we have gone
To the famed Houndslow Heath,
Though an unwelcome guest
To the minions of fortune
My Bonnie Black Bess.

So gentle you have stood
When the coaches we would stop.
The money and the jewelry
Down to me they would drop.

We would never rob a poor man
Or ever oppress,
Any widows or orphans,
My Bonnie Black Bess.

When auger-eyed justice
Did me hot pursue
From Yorktown to London
Like lightning we flew.
No toll-gates would stop us
High waters you would breast
In eight hours you made it
My Bonnie Black Bess.

Hark, Hark! The blood-hounds are approaching
But they never shall take
A dumb friend like you
So noble and great.
To save me, my dumb friend,
You have done your best.
Thou art worn-out and weary,
My Bonnie Black Bess.

Now hate gathers o'er me
Despair is my lot
And the law does pursue me
For the many I've shot.

Some will pity,
While they all must confess
It's through kindness I kill you,
My Bonnie Black Bess.

No one can ever say
Ingratitude dwelt
In the bosom of Turpin,
A vice never felt.
We will both die together
And soon be at rest
There, there! I have shot you
My Bonnie Black Bess.

In years after years
When I am gone
This story will be handed
From father to son.
I will die like a man
And soon be at rest
So fare you well forever
My Bonnie Black Bess.

With the Cherrycows, Jess Fears was our ballad-singer. All the old ones, all the sad ones, were known to him; and the saddest was:

BILLY VENIRO

Billy Veniro heard them say
In an Arizona town one day
That a band of Apache Indians
Were on the trail of death;
He heard them tell of murder done,
Of the men killed at Rocky Run.
"There is danger at the cow-ranch!"
Veniro cried beneath his breath.

On a ranch forty miles
In a little place that lay
In a green and shady valley
In a mighty wilderness.
Half a score of homes were there
And in one a maiden fair
Held the heart of Billy Veniro
Veniro's little Bess.

So no wonder he grew pale
When he heard the cowboy's tale
Tell of those men seen murdered
The day before at Rocky Run.
"As sure as there is a God above
I will save the girl I love.
By my love for little Bessie
I must see there is something done."

119

When his brave resolve was made
Not a moment more he stayed.
"Why, my man," his comrades told him
When they heard his daring plan,
"You are riding straight to death."
But he answered: "Hold your breath.
I may never reach the cow-ranch
Though I do the best I can."

As he crossed the alkali bed
And his thoughts flew on ahead
To the little band at the cow-ranch
Thinking not of danger near,
With his quirt's unceasing whirl
And the jingle of his spurs
Little brown Chapo bore the cowboy
Far away from a far frontier.

Lower and lower sank the sun
He drew rein at Rocky Run.
"Here those men met death, my Chapo,"
And he stroked his horse's mane.
"And with them we will go, too,
E'er the breaking of the morn.
If I fail, God bless my Bessie!"
And he started out again.

Sharp and keen, a rifle shot
Woke the echoes of the spot.
"I am wounded!" cried Veniro
As he swayed from side to side.
"Where there is life there is always hope
Onward slowly I will lope
If I never reach the cow-ranch
Bessie Dear shall know I tried.

"I will save her yet!" he cried,
"Bessie Lee shall know I died,
For her sake!" And then he halted
In the shadow of a hill.
From a branch a twig he broke
And he dipped his pen of oak
In the warm blood that was spurting
From the wound above his heart.

From his shaps he took
With weak hand a little book
Tore a blank leaf from it
Saying: "This shall be my will."
He arose and wrote: "Too late.
Apache warriors lay in wait.
Good-by, Bessie, God bless you darling."
And he felt the warm blood start.

121

Then he made his message fast,
Love's first letter and its last.
To the saddle horn he tied it
While his lips were white with pain.
"Take this message, if not me,
To little Bess," said he.
Then he tied himself to the saddle
And gave his horse the reins.

Just at dusk a horse of brown
Wet with sweat came panting down
Through the little lane at the cow-ranch
And stopped at Bessie's door.
But the cowboy was asleep
And his slumbers were so deep
That little Bess could not awake him,
Though she tried forevermore.

Now you have heard this story told
By the young and by the old,
Way down there at the cow-ranch
The night the Apaches came.
Heard them speak of the bloody fight
How the chief fell in the flight
And of those panic-stricken warriors
When they speak Veniro's name.

This is a true Western ballad—and there are others, like "California Joe," that would take half an hour to sing—but one of Jess's favorites, a song very near to cowboy hearts, was:

WHEN WORK IS DONE THIS FALL

A jolly group of cowboys
    discussing their plans one day
When one says, "I will tell you something, boys,
    before I'm gone away.
I am a cowboy as you see, although
    I am dressed in rags,
I used to be a wild one a taking on big jags.

"I have a home, boys, a good one you all know,
Although I have not seen it since long ago.
I am going back to Dixie
    once for to see them all,
I am going back to Dixie to see my mother
    when work is done this fall.

"After the round-ups are over,
    after the shipping is done
I am going to see my mother
    before my money is all gone.

123

My mother's heart is breaking,
    breaking for me and that's all.
And with God's help I will see her
    when work is done this fall."

That very same night this poor cowboy
    went out to stand his guard.
The wind was blowing fiercely
    and the rain was falling hard.
The cattle they got frightened
    and ran in a mad stampede.
Poor boy, he tried to head them
    while riding at full speed.

Riding in the darkness
    so loudly he did shout.
A trying to head the cattle,
    a trying to turn them about.
When his saddled night-horse stumbled
    and upon him did fall,
Now the poor boy will not see his mother
    when work is done this fall.

We picked him up so gently
    and laid him on his bed
A standing all around the poor cowboy,
    a thinking he was dead.

When he opened wide his blue eyes,
　　looked all around and said,
"Boys, I think those are the last steers
　　I shall ever head.

"So Bill, you take my saddle
　　and Charlie, you take my bed
And George, you take my six-shooter
　　and be sure that I am dead.
I am going to a new range
　　for I hear my Master's call
And I will not see my mother
　　when work is done this fall.

"After the round-ups were over,
　　after the shipping was all done
I was going to see my mother
　　before my money was all gone.
My mother's heart is breaking,
　　breaking for me and that's all.
And if God had a spared my absence
　　I would have seen her
When work was done this fall."

But a cowboy has got to laugh or he couldn't stand the racket, and Outlaw Tom had a good one. All shot to pieces for meter and rhythm, but what is left is the real thing.

The Horse Wrangler

One spring I thought, jest for fun,
I would try cow punching
Jest to see how it was done.

I tackled Cattle King
He said: "My foreman is in town,
He's down at the hog-ranch
And easy found."

The next day, going out with Brown
He augered me all the way,
Telling me the work
Was nothing but play.

But oh, how that son-of-a-witch did lie!
The bastard had his gall.
He put me in charge of a cavvyard
Of a hundred and sixty head.
When one got away
Brown's head turned red.

They saddled me up an old gray hack
With sixteen set-fasts on his back
Using gunnysacks to pad it up
Which took my bedding all.

I got up on that old gray horse
He jumped and turned around
And when he hit the ground—Oh Gawd!
But I shot on like a cannonball
Till the earth come in my way.

They took me into camp
And rubbed me down with a picket-pin.
"You are doing well," said Brown.
"In the morning, if you don't die,
I'll give you another horse to try."

Says I to Brown: "Can't I walk?"
"Yes," says Brown. "To town."

So my friends if you ever think
Of trying a cowboy's life
Get a heavy insurance upon your life
Kiss your mother, your sister and your wife
And cut your throat with an old, dull knife.

Another good laugh is on the cowboy that
hangs around town, a kind of Main Street cowboy, chiefly interested in bumming a drink.

THE TOP SCREW

While you are all so frisky
I will sing you a song.
I will take a horn of whiskey
To help the sing along.
It is all about a top screw
When he is busted flat
Setting around town
With his Mexican hat.

See him setting around
With a crowd he thinks he knows
He is smoking cigarettes
And smoking through his nose.
He will tell you in a moment
That he owns a certain brand
And he will lead you to believe
That he is a daisy hand.

Put him on a pony
He will do good work
But down in the branding pen
He is dam sure to shirk.
With a natural-leaf tobacco
In the pocket of his vest
He will tell you that his eight
Dollar pants is the best.

Put him on herd
He will ring all day;
If anything gets out
It is sure to get away;
If anything is missing
He will lay it to the screws
And he will swear the lazy devils
Was trying to take a snooze.

When he strikes a greener
He is dam sure to start a rig
He will put him on the chuck-box
And make him dance a jig.
He will wave a loaded six-shooter
And he will make him step about.
He is a regular Ben Thompson
When the boss is not about.

This is all about
A trip up the trail
I will lead you clean to Kansas
To finish up my tale.
He wants to be a top man
With nothing much to do
And he will tell you about him
Chasing off the wild Sioux.

He is going to Montana,
He is going to make a raise,
He is good for a hundred dollars a month
The balance of his days;
Just to show you
That he don't care for expense
He tears down the bushes
With his eight dollar pants.

But the cowboy's deepest mood is one of
melancholy and discontent and, after the rollicking songs are all over, in the solemn watches
of the night, someone will start singing "The
Lament." It is an old, old song, with many
variations. This short one I got from Jess Fears.

A Cowboy's Lament

As I rode down the streets of Laredo
So early one day it was there I espied
A handsome young cowboy
    all clothed in white linen
Clothed in white linen
    and dressed for the grave.

Chorus:

> Oh play your fife lowly
>> and beat your drum slowly
> And play the Death March
>> as you carry me along.
> Go take me to the graveyard
>> and place the sod o'er me
> For I'm a young cowboy
>> and I know I've done wrong.

It was once in the saddle I used to go dashing,
It was once in the saddle I used to be gay;
I first took to drinking, then to card-playing,
Got shot through the body, I'm dying today.

Go gather a group of young cowboys around you
And tell them the story of this, my sad fate.
Tell them to stop their deep drinking
And all their wild ways before it's too late.

Go write a letter to my gray-haired mother
And break the news gently to sister so dear.
But still there's another even dearer than mother
Who will weep bitter tears
>> when she knows I am here.

131

"Oh, give me a cup of cold water,
A cup of cold water," the poor fellow cried,
When I returned the spirit had departed
And gone to its Giver—the cowboy had died.

Chorus:

So play your fife lowly
    and beat your drum slowly
And play the Death March
    as you carry me along.
Go take me to the graveyard
    and place the sod o'er me
For I'm a young cowboy
    and I know I've done wrong.

CHAPTER IX

COWBOY FRIENDS

THIS boy, Jess Fears, was the best type of Texas cowboy, raised in the old traditions. He had had an uncle in the Texas Rangers and possessed the steadfast courage of that band of fearless fighters who guarded the last frontier. He ran away from home at the age of eleven and worked for several big outfits until he became a top hand. When he was breaking a bronk he had a line of talk that seemed to take all the fight out of him, but when it came to riding them he threw the reins on their necks. And all the time he would laugh.

"Ah-hah-hah—hah-hah-hah! I know you're a snake. Everybody knows it. But you don't look bad to me. Ah-hah-hah-hah—you look good to me. Make a nice work-horse. The more we get acquainted the better I like you. *You* ain't so bad—your mammy gives milk."

It was a very convincing patter, though no better than Rusty Bill Rustin's.

"Well, here's leetle Black Reever! He's a pretty leetle hawse too, and gentle. Oh, hell no, he wouldn't kick anybody. He remembers old Beel, don't you, Black Reever? He remembers the good time I give him, down at Safford. Sure he's gentle—I broke him myself."

They made a great pair, these top hands on the Cherrycow; but, off by himself, Jess spoke often of his old pardner and friend, Montana Bill, who had recently died of pneumonia. They had broken horses together at Safford, and Miller had a pair of Angora shaps of which he was very proud. They had belonged to a Montana friend of his, who had been killed by the fall of a horse. Some people were superstitious about them and, when Bill offered Jess the shaps shortly before his death, he declined them. Miller gave them to another friend, who wore them into Willcox, got kicked in the stomach by a horse and died within a week. Jess believes that, if he had accepted them, he would have been the man to get killed, and he stayed with his old bull's-hide leggings.

Before Bill Miller came to Safford he had been a Grand Canyon guide at El Tovar, making seventy-five dollars a month in pay and tips, and breaking mules on the side. He was sitting pretty when two Eastern schoolma'ams came along and got him fired off the job. Nothing suited these ladies—their stirrups were too long, the saddles were not right, and the mules were positively dangerous; and they asked so many questions that Bill was worn clear out.

At the foot of the first long pitch down the Canyon there is a geodetic survey monument, surmounted by a pile of rocks; and the elder of the teachers asked who had died there. Bill said it was a guide. Sure, he was taking two old maids down the Canyon and they talked him to death. He just stepped off the trail and fell dead. This made the ladies sore and they stopped talking for a while. Then they asked him to sing a cowboy song and he refused.

That shut them up, which was what Bill

wanted; but back at the hotel they decided to forgive him and one gave him a ten-cent tip. Miller spit on the dime and threw it into the Grand Canyon of Arizona, for which he was very properly fired. With his pardner, Buckskin Charley, Bill went on a big drunk from which they still date time at El Tovar. After shooting off four or five boxes of cartridges without getting a rise out of the local officer they accidentally set the hay of their bed afire and ended by burning down their tent and leaving the corral a wreck.

Such volcanic natures as these were common in the days before the war, but none of them could match Paul and Rowdy, the Texas fighting fools. Working cattle was too slow for them and they finally found their sphere "moving sheep." There are very few Western cowboys who have not, at some time in their career, moved sheep off the Boss's range, but Paul and Rowdy made a business of it. They went into a country where a sheep-war was going on and, against all the fighting Mexicans that the sheepmen could hire, they moved them and kept them moved.

This can be done very simply by the right kind of a man by just riding up to the Mexicans, informing them they are trespassing and pointing to the shortest way home. Or it can be done as Paul and Rowdy loved to do it, by shooting up their camps at night and running them out of the country. For this and other offenses against the law they were compelled to leave the State, but when the United States entered the World War and called for volunteers they returned, stood trial and "came clear."

Within a month after they had entered training camp each boasted that he "whipped his louie," a serious breach of discipline at any time but doubly so in time of war. For this offense they could have been sent to a military prison, but the grim old Army officers in charge of their camp chose to regard the matter differently. Instead of committing them in disgrace to Fort Leavenworth they made them first sergeants and sent them to the front. They were the stuff that good soldiers are made of, and each lived up to the part.

Rowdy, the fighting fool, was made wagon-master of an ammunition train, entrusted with the important duty of rushing ammunition to the front. But, during a night attack when the enemy planes were bombing the roads, he rode ahead to inspect a bad crossing and, instead of his wagons, they got him. He was blown to bits and when Paul heard the news he deserted to find the body of his friend.

After being absent without leave for ten days he returned and reported for duty; and again, miraculously, the grim Army officers dismissed all charges against him. In battle after battle he served as a sharpshooter or in running messages under fire; and when, gassed and wounded, he came back to Arizona, he found himself a hero. The citizens who had formerly clamored for his arrest assembled to do him honor, and today he occupies a position of responsibility and trust. On the Apache Reservation in 1909, he and the men about him recognized only the Law of the Range—unquestioning obedience to the boss.

Dad Hardiman was tall and gangling, with a head as round and shining as a billiard-ball; but he was a wagon-boss of the old Texas school, and accustomed to handling hard men. The top hands kidded him, but they obeyed his orders; and the others followed suit. Dad did not hang around—he gave his orders and went away—so the cowboys did the work. But there was one man in the outfit who was bad, and wanted everybody to know it. He always wore his gun, even when they were working in the corral, and we called him Rang Tang Bill.

Bill was built along the lines of a gorilla, with big hands that hung to his knees; but he had a bad habit of "sleeping on his hand"—so it would slip and wake him up—and several horses were lost on his guard. Or that was the way Pecos doped it out; and when, one morning, his whole string turned up missing, he roped out Rang Tang's top horse.

This was against all round-up practice and Rang Tang came over on the run, but when he began to shout Pecos swung his mount around and pointed to the C on its hip.

"You see that brand?" he asked. "This is a Cherrycow horse, and as long as I'm working for the Company I don't figure on going afoot. You've been sleeping on your elbow, you old so-and-so, and—what are you going to do about it?"

He reached over and pulled Bill's long nose, but Rang Tang had heard about the slender pistol which Pecos was supposed to carry in his boot, and he decided not to do anything. Pecos came from a fighting family, and he wouldn't have made that play unless he was all set to shoot. He was under bonds to keep the peace, and under court orders not to carry a gun; but they were out in the middle of the Apache Reservation and Rang Tang had to back down.

Dad Hardiman sent two men to trail the strays, and they brought Pecos' lost horses back; but after that he kept crowding Rang Tang, and it looked as if they would fight. Pecos was a man of quick decisions and unquestioned courage; and on their way down to Black River Crossing, when his horse got away, he had shown what he could do. He had stepped off to shoot a deer

140

when his mount broke and ran. Several men took after it, over a very rough country, but Pecos whipped up his carbine and knocked it down the first shot.

He knew that a cowboy without a saddle was of no further use to the boss, and of course the Company had more horses; but he was just as quick to rope one of Bill's when he found his own horses were lost. Only a few days later Cherrycow Charley lost *his* saddle, and he had to draw his pay. He borrowed another man's horse to chase this recreant steed, which had thrown him off in the rocks; but when he came back without it, the wagon-boss paid him off.

"Well, anyhow," said Charley, "the crazy bastard will die—he'll never git that saddle off. The hind cinch was fastened with a buckle and he'll drag it till he dies."

This was a small revenge for the loss of his saddle, and the chances are he was wrong. Some hidden Apache, watching the race from afar, would get horse and saddle that same night. Charley was no great loss, for the round-up was nearly over and he had never been much of a

hand; and Pecos was working on Rang Tang
Bill, to make *him* swell up and quit. But Rang
Tang, though he had the head of an ape, was
smarter than we thought. He stood the gaff;
and, when he did quit, a few months later he
had all the money in the outfit. And he never
paid it back.

Pecos had a wife and family, down on the
Gila; and every time we got within twenty miles
he would take a chunk of beef and ride home
"to get a change of clothes." It was a great
phrase with him, and he used it to the limit on
Bill, who had not done so well. He had married
a woman up at Globe who, after getting all his
money and worldly goods, had gone back to
Joplin, Missouri. Everybody but Bill knew that
she had quit him cold; and Pecos was always
rubbing it in about his having to go to Joplin,
Missouri, to get a change of clothes.

But one day Bill, who had been working at a
station, rode in on the outfit wild-eyed, his
upper lip swelled up like a muley cow's.

"Hydrophobia!" he said. "I was bit by a
hydrophobia skunk."

Now nobody liked Rang Tang and some positively hated him; but they couldn't stand by
and see a fellow-man go to his death from rabies.
A year or two before two cowboys had been bit,
and they had taken up a collection to send them
to the Pasteur Institute, at Chicago. One had
gone right through and got his treatment; but
the other stopped off in Kansas to try a mad-
stone, and he had died a horrible death. So they
all chipped in a month's pay and put Rang
Tang Bill on the train for Chicago; only to
hear, a few months later, that he had played
them a dirty trick. He had scratched his lip
with a brass pin to give it that hydrophobia
look; and when he wrote back he reported that
he had stopped off at Joplin, Missouri, to get a
change of clothes.

CHAPTER X

SHIPPING OUT

THEY were a great bunch of rough-joshers, these cowboys; and the butts of many a joke were Bishop and Kinch, the Mormons. Or at least the boys claimed they were Mormons—Jack Mormons, anyway. Mormons when they were at home, and something else out on the range. They were always feeling of Bob's red head, upon which they professed to find "bishop's horns," sure sign he was going to be a bishop of the Church and have at least four wives.

"Aw," he would say, "you boys are jealous." And come back with some joke of his own, with many allusions to Bugscuffle, Texas. This was a legendary town, to which they referred all big liars; and from there they would proceed to Ticklegrass Canyon, another liar's paradise.

"Oh, he's from Bugscuffle," they would say;

and the man whose veracity had been questioned would answer back:

"No, suh! I come from that big, black canyon, away over on the other side."

"Oh, you mean Ticklegrass Canyon. I was through there once, and the grass had drifted in until it was a hundred feet deep. Never did git all them stickers out of my clothes—but what was *you* doing there?"

"That's just what the sheriff wanted to know, when he finally caught up with me. He was riding the best hawse in the county, barring one, and he made it from where we started in eighteen hours and twenty-two minutes. I made it in eighteen flat."

There were a thousand other jokes about men who had beat the sheriff to the line, and many more sly remarks about how come they had stolen that horse.

"I was walking along one day when I see a nice new rope in the road, and I says to myself:

" 'I'd better pick that up and take it along or some son-of-a-goat might *steal* it.'

"Well, suh, believe it or not, when I got back

146

home there was a *hawse* on the other end of it. Now I knowed them ornery neighbors of mine wouldn't believe that that was an accident, so I stepped up on the hawse and come out to New Mexico."

But sooner or later they would get back to the Mormons, until Bishop Greenhouse pulled a good one that finally shut them up. It went off something like this.

"Mighty funny about these Tee-hannos," he observed. "They say, back in Texas, when a man gits where he can count fifty they set him to teaching school—and when he can count a hundred he gits onto himself and leaves the cussed country. Ordinary folks kin only count to twenty—ten fingers and ten toes, like an Injun. It's sure a fine country to come away from."

He glanced over at Kinch Talley who nodded, not being much on talk, and Buck Buchanan took up the cudgels for Texas.

"They tell me, Bob," he said, "that them Mormons down on the river can't talk no more —jest git along by signs and a kind of sheep-blat they have."

147

"Nope," answered Greenhouse, "they is such people, but they don't live along the Heely. Them fellers you're thinking of is in the goat business. They don't say *baaa* like a sheep; they go *maaa* like a goat. I've heeard tell of them, too. It seems they don't wear no pants—nothing but shirts—and when they have a dance the gals have to tie a red rag on their big toe, so they can tell 'em apart. They live on them goat ranches, back in Western Texas."

He paused and looked about triumphantly, but only Kinch Talley laughed.

"I was driving a bunch of strays through that Mormon country," explained Buck Buchanan. "That's where I got the idee. That's a great country, ain't it, Bishop? Lots of houses, too. I remember I stopped one time at a street crossing, and there was houses on all four corners. They was a lot of kids playing around, and I asked one of them whose houses they were, and he says:

" 'My father's.'

" 'How come your father has so many?' I says. 'Does he rent 'em?'

148

" 'No sir,' the kid says, 'he lives in 'em. Don't you know him? He's the bishop!' "

There was a roar of laughter at this unkind jest, but Bishop had become accustomed to it.

"Aw, you're jest jealous," he grunted, and let them holler awhile, until he finally got back the lead.

"That's one thing you'll never find around a Mormon town," he said, "you'll never find no Texicans. Of course a Mormon has to work, and that bars most of them at the start. But I don't know, seems like the first settlers took a prejudice agin' 'em. I remember my old man telling how it come that way. Course they must be mistaken, but the Mormons think a Texan ain't got no sense.

"The Mormons was the first people to settle along the Heely, and my grandpaw was one of the leaders. He killed a lot of Injuns, believe me! But one day, when he was gitting kind of old and feeble-like, he got a notion into his head that he wanted a squirrel-skin, and so he called in my father and said:

" 'Son, you take your rifle and ride up on the

149

peaks and git me a gray tree-squirrel; and be careful not to shoot him in the head, because I want the brains to tan the skin with.'

"So my father he went up in the pines and hunted around; but the only gray squirrel he could find was sticking his head over a limb, and rather than not git nothing he shot him anyhow. Well, he brought it back and said to the old man:

" 'I'm mighty sorry, Dad. The squirrels was awful scarce and, rather than not git any, I had to shoot this one through the head.'

" 'Oh, that's all right,' the old man says. 'You got a nice skin, anyway, and I reckon we can fix it somehow. I tell you what you do! They's a bunch of Texans camped down on the lower water—you go down and kill one of them, and mebby we can use *his* brains.' "

Greenhouse paused and looked around with squinched-up, twinkling eyes; and at last Buck Buchanan broke the silence.

"Well," he demanded roughly, "what's the joke?"

"Well, sir," ran on the Bishop, "you wouldn't

hardly believe it, but my old man told me he had to kill six of them Texicans to git brains enough to tan that squirrel-skin! That's why they won't take 'em into the Church!''

There was a near-riot after that; but the Texans, like Bishop, were accustomed to taking hot ones, and they were giving off at the head mightily when we took the long trail for the Gila River and Bylas, where we were due to ship the beef-herd. Some of the biggest lies of the trip were being told and their language was something frightful when, down the road towards San Carlos, a canvas-topped buggy appeared and the cook began to curse. It was Morton, the Range Boss, who stayed in town most of the time while he carried on the "book business" of the Company, and Sam was not alone in his sentiments.

To the cowboys, that covered buggy brought up memories of the worst kind; for Morton, who had been a humble "wolfer," or wolf-trapper, had married a local school-teacher and they knew he was bringing his wife. Otherwise he would come on a horse, like a cowboy, which they stated emphatically he was not. But his wife had been the making of Morton and he liked to take her with him. She was a woman of great ambitions for her husband and, first of all, she had got busy on his diction, while all the cowboys laughed.

For months, for years, she had taught him to speak another language—the language of *her* world, where nobody ever swore or used low words. It was the joke of the countryside until Henry Boice came along, after buying out Vickers, and made him boss over them all. He needed an educated man, to keep his books and handle his affairs, and Morton could qualify on that; but the reason he had got the job was that he never smoked, drank, or swore. And Boice never smoked, drank or swore. He was a man of stern moral convictions and it seemed almost providential to find another man of his kind.

So Morton was the Range Boss now—next to Boice—and it was a pleasure to listen to his soft, cultured accents; but the boys could never get over it. Here Dad Hardiman and his cowboys did all the dirty work—swimming rivers, moving the cattle, fighting off the Apaches—while

Morton for double the money lived in a good house in town and seldom appeared on the range. But there was a reason for that, as I soon found out when Sam warmed up to the subject. Mr. Morton was not popular with the rough-scuff cowboys—and his schoolma'am wife was pisen. Not satisfied with educating her husband and seeing him made boss of the range, she had taken it upon herself to extend this sweet, womanly influence to others not so apt. In fact—and here Sam swelled up and hissed like a Gila monster—she had even had the nerve to correct the language of the *cook*. The former cook.

Yes sir, while the outfit was working day and night, she had appeared in this same covered buggy, which even now was toiling up the road, and camped on the cook for a week. He was a patient, obliging soul and when the Range Boss drove in he had made the lady welcome. To be sure it spoiled everything, as far as the cowboys were concerned, to have a woman around; but *cusi* had accepted her as one thing more, and they had to cut out the cussing. But when, the first morning, he had hollered:

"Come and git it!" Mrs. Morton had not

come. She stepped out of her tent several hours later, after the cowboys had had their breakfast and gone, so it was necessary to begin all over again and cook her another breakfast. Having risen so late she was not sufficiently hungry to eat when they came in at noon. The result was the cook found himself preparing two sets of meals three times a day, in the midst of other onerous duties; but he stood up to it until she corrected his English, when he quit.

He told the Range Boss, the Straw Boss, and all of them that he was not hired to cook for women; and especially for a schoolma'am, who was not satisfied with his grammar. So he threw up the job, and the cowboys had had six weeks of misery while they ate after Cherrycow Charley. It had taken Morton a long time to find a new cook, and Sam intimated broadly that, at the first word from *her,* Mort would have to start in all over again. Then he shut up, and when the covered buggy arrived nobody spoke a word.

It was noon and the cowboys were sitting in the dirt, eating; and at the thought of all the trouble she had caused them they responded

UPPER—
   The horseherd was driven across the Gila first, to
   pack down the treacherous quicksands.

LOWER—
   The cattle spread out along the boggy river and drank.
   (*Photographs by Dane Coolidge*)

Young Apache Brave, Hog-Fat from Eating Company Beef.

(Photograph by Dune Coolidge)

very briefly to her greetings. As for Sam, his face was black with rage, and he let her husband do all the rustling when she asked for a little "lunch." That was what they called it, these school-teachers—anything in the middle of the day—and at night it was always dinner, whether they had had dinner at noon or not. But Sam was determined not to be called down by no schoolma'am, and she soon saw she had got in wrong.

They drove out to the herd and circled back to town, and Sam notified the wagon boss that when she came back he quit. He would have troubles enough down on the river, cooking for cattle-buyers and people from town, without catering to *her;* and the word must have got back to the Range Boss, for after that he rode out alone.

We got in late, after a dry drive to Gila Crossing, and Dad sent the horse-herd over first to tramp down the treacherous quicksand. Then the cattle spread out along the river and drank.

We camped that evening at a deserted house, a few miles down the river from San Carlos, and

I was surprised to learn it had recently been the headquarters of an extensive Indian Farm. The Apaches had had little fields and gardens clear up the river to the fort, where they raised corn and beans and watermelons; but an obliging Agent had turned the whole river-bottom over to the Company. This Agent, so I was told, was an old Army Officer who believed the only good Indians were dead ones; and furthermore that the Apaches were not an agricultural people anyway and there was no use trying to teach them.

So the Indian Farmer's house was now vacant, though Boice had had nothing to do with it; and the big, fenced field came in handy to hold the horses while the cowboys were night-guarding the beef-herd.

The Apaches were camped on the barren mesa, a mile or more from the river, and the next morning I rode out to see them. The bucks were hog-fat and playing monte for big money, dollars being strewn all over the blanket, but the children were sore-eyed and dirty and the women kept out of sight. I was about as welcome as a rattlesnake in a dog-town, but finally hired a gambler who was broke to pose for me and he poured the Indians' woes into my ears.

All their nice farms had been taken away from them. The women had to carry water on their heads for miles. The Company had brought in cattle and pastured them in their fields; the Indians had to wear brass tags, like dogs. Their men, who had been warriors, were not allowed to possess guns, except .22 rifles to shoot rabbits; and if they were caught out on the Reservation without a permit they could never go any more. Thousands of cattle were pastured on their Reservation, and the Company paid a dollar a head. But the Agent never gave them any of the money—it was all kept back in Washington.

His story was so long and his complaints so numerous that I felt almost sorry for him. Almost—for the Apaches of those early days were the most hateful Indians in the West. The bucks who sat around had a mean, vindictive look; and when they gazed down on the river, where the cowboys were rounding up the cattle, I felt it was time to go. These cattle were a herd of eighteen hundred spayed heifers which had been turned into the Indians' fields, and they should have been glad to get rid of them. But they were not.

There was something wrong somewhere, but it was not what I thought it was. Of the eighteen hundred heifers, less than eight hundred were rounded up. The rest had been driven into the hills at night and butchered by these same complaining Indians, and what they were mad about was that they had not got them all. The trader at San Carlos informed me that all he sold these Apaches was rope, butcher-knives and salt; so I decided to quit worrying about them. They could take care of themselves without any outside assistance, and from the number of Mexican dollars which I saw on the blanket I judged they were selling the jerked beef.

The next morning Henry Boice arrived in response to a wire from Dad and, while the beef-herd was being punched into the cars, he ordered another round-up. He had had two men riding herd over these heifers ever since he had taken over the outfit, and he could not believe that the Indians had run off so many. The river-bottom was very brushy, there was a rocky mountain to the west; but it did not seem reasonable that, so near the fort, they could get away with half his herd.

Classing the cattle in the corrals and driving them up the chutes was a long and tedious job; and so, not to seem too inquisitive about other people's business, I rode down the river to get some pictures of Bylas, the Coyotero chief. He was an old-time Apache with his shirt-tail out and a breech-clout under his pants—the only Indian to cling to his land when the white men ordered them off. He had been bludgeoned over the head with a six-shooter; but he had stayed, and kept his fields.

What I liked about him most was that he made no mouthy complaints, but posed for his picture like a gentleman, holding the reins above his plow. He was proud of the fact that he had given up the war-path and devoted himself to the agriculture which the Agent had said he wasn't adapted to.

"Chief Bylas work. Yes," he said. "Other In-

159

juns no good. Allee time gamble, gamble!" he made the motions of dealing cards. "Allee time ride horse around"—he forked two fingers over his other hand and jogged them up and down. "Allee time sleep"—he leaned his head on one hand. "Bymby hungry. Come to Chief Bylas. Say—'Me hungry, you gimme maize.' Young Injun no good. Me work."

I expressed my appreciation of his industry and thrift and he launched forth as follows:

"Me big chief. Chief Bylas. Washingtone know me. *Viente-quatro* [34] years *pasado* me go see him. Ten days, ten night, ride on train allee time. Come to New Orleans—big town. Then go to Washingtone. Big house—white. Good. Washingtone good man—gimme clothes, gimme grub. He say he Injun's friend. One moon I stay—then come home. Me be good man now. Me work!"

I shook hands with this honest Indian who was not afraid to work and went back to where the cowboys were still loading cattle, while a big bunch of Apaches looked on. When the railroad had been built through their Reservation

CHIEF BYLAS, OF THE COYOTERO APACHES,
gives up being a warrior and starts to plough. The Chief is holding the reins.

(Photograph by Dane Coolidge)

A Long Row of Apaches,
like crows along a slaughter house fence, watching all that good beef leave the country.

(Photograph by Dane Coolidge)

they had held out for free rides on all freight trains, and for many months they had trundled back and forth until the novelty of the thing wore off. But news of the cattle shipments had brought them all down again and they sat in long rows looking on, like crows along a slaughter-house fence.

Perhaps they hoped that some steer would break a leg and there would be a little free beef; but when the second round-up came in with only seven more heifers their hopes were definitely off. Mr. Boice had proved beyond the shadow of a doubt that the Indians around San Carlos had stolen over a thousand fat cows. They had got more in proportion than their brothers at Fort Apache, and his answer to them was the same.

"Round up all these cattle along the river," he said, "and push them out on the Reservation. If I've got to keep these Indians in beef I'm going to make them work for it."

That was one thing the cowboys liked about Henry S. Boice, in spite of his being a reformer. He knew how to take a loss, and what to do

161

about it. He was
game sport, b
them. Bec
sell wh
Reservation.
that drink for w

It was quite a prob
it. The next day he shipp
load of cattle, and as he swung
with a sigh:

"The school-teachers and reformers a
closing in on us. Have to go to Kansas Cit,
Missouri, to get a drink of whiskey."

THE END

162